FOUNDER, FARMER, TINKER, THIEF

FOUNDER, FARMER, TINKER, THIEF

THE FOUR PHASES OF THE ENTREPRENEUR'S JOURNEY

CHRIS COOPER

TWOBRAIN MEDIA

COPYRIGHT © 2019 CHRIS COOPER

FOUNDER, FARMER, TINKER, THIEF
The Four Phases of the Entrepreneur's Journey

ISBN   978-1-5445-0151-2 *Hardcover*

978-1-5445-0149-9 *Paperback*

978-1-5445-0150-5 *Ebook*

978-1-5445-0341-7 *Audiobook*

CONTENTS

FOREWORD

What do you want to be when your business grows up?

I ask because many entrepreneurs don't think beyond the present. Obsessed with pleasing the next customer, making the next deadline, or finding the missing receipt at month's end, passionate, motivated owners sometimes forget that a business is either shrinking or growing at all times, creating larger challenges.

Losses require courage and quick, decisive action, while profits require vision, foresight, and careful planning for the future. In both situations, the business is evolving each day, and it takes a strong leader to guide it. But to lead, a person must have a destination, and many do not yet look to the horizon.

Entrepreneurship is hard work, and the character of the average small business owner might be part of the problem. A strong willingness to roll up the sleeves and do everything can doom an owner to a life of twelve-hour days that start with customer service and end with a plunger in a toilet. It's the curse of the talented. Their skill in keeping the ship afloat means they often don't look beyond the bow.

Too often, I've watched gloriously talented and incredibly passionate people burn themselves out or struggle to turn a profit. In other cases, businesses grow but stall, leaving the owners confused and frustrated. And some people simply don't know what to do with success and aren't prepared to seize the day when it arrives.

It doesn't have to be that way.

A path exists from a passionate business founder to a farmer who grows a profitable business that provides opportunities for others and better service to clients. A good farmer becomes a tinker whose success has freed him or her to take assertive steps that move an enterprise from small to medium. Beyond those roles is that of the thief: a successful, visionary owner who essentially retires to focus on leveraging connections to reach other industries and build a legacy—something that improves the world and lives on beyond the owner.

This path creates a "perfect day" for an owner who has worked hard but smart to earn success and freedom. While the bright-eyed founder and the salt-of-the-earth farmer might imagine these rewards and feel guilty for desiring them, tinkers and thieves know that their success has created a ripple effect. In their wake are new founders and farmers who are working toward their own perfect days thanks to the inspiration provided by the tinkers and the mentorship supplied by the thieves.

I'm walking this path just like you are. I've worked sixteen-hour days, canceled vacations, and headed to our business before 5 a.m. to patch cracks in drywall. When I reached the end of my rope, I talked to Chris Cooper and the Two-Brain Business mentors who helped me refocus my business. Chris and his team asked me what I wanted to be when our small gym outgrew the hobby stage, and they taught me to see the business not as a labor of love but as an asset that can help me live the life I want.

My wife and I aren't even close to the Thief stage yet, but we're moving ever closer to our perfect day because we have a dream, a solid plan, and a support network. We know where we are, and we know where we want to go.

This book will help you learn whether you're a founder, farmer, tinker, or thief, and it will help you become better in your current role as you work to move on to the next.

You'll find your own path to success and blaze a trail for others to follow. You'll become a better business owner, you'll have happier staff members and clients, and you'll have more free time to enjoy your success with your family.

So what do you want to be when your business grows up?

—MIKE WARKENTIN
FOUNDER/FARMER
CROSSFIT 204

COME my tan-faced children,
Follow well in order, get your weapons ready,
Have you your pistols? Have you
    your sharp-edged axes?
Pioneers! O pioneers!

We detachments steady throwing,
Down the edges, through the passes, up
    the mountains steep,
Conquering, holding, daring, venturing
    as we go the unknown ways,
Pioneers! O pioneers!

We primeval forests felling,
We the rivers stemming, vexing we and
    piercing deep the mines within,
We the surface broad surveying, we
    the virgin soil upheaving,
Pioneers! O pioneers!

Life's involv'd and varied pageants,
All the forms and shows, all the workmen at their work,
All the seamen and the landsmen, all
    the masters with their slaves,
Pioneers! O pioneers!

From Nebraska, from Arkansas,
Central inland race are we, from Missouri, with
     the continental blood intervein'd,
All the hands of comrades clasping, all
     the Southern, all the Northern,
Pioneers! O pioneers!

Have the elder races halted?
Do they droop and end their lesson, wearied
     over there beyond the seas?
We take up the task eternal, and the
     burden and the lesson,
Pioneers! O pioneers!

O resistless restless race!
O beloved race in all! O my breast aches
     with tender love for all!
O I mourn and yet exult, I am rapt with love for all,
Pioneers! O pioneers!

—WALT WHITMAN, "PIONEERS! O PIONEERS!" 1865

PREFACE

This book is about entrepreneurship. More specifically, it's a map to the four stages of business ownership.

First, the Founder phase. Heady with his big idea, an entrepreneur takes his shaky first steps toward self-sustainability. This stage, more than any other, is romantically idealized by movie, book, and hashtag. It is denoted by innovation. The new founder imagines himself "building his wings on the way down," and doing all the #grinding and #hustling he sees from his heroes. But eventually, once the trees have been felled and the cliffs have been scaled and after trying every possible path, the founder must shift from innovator to cultivator. She must transition to the next phase of entrepreneurship to succeed.

Next is the Farmer phase. Here, the entrepreneur works to create a cycle of predictable harvest. He builds systems and policies. He hires staff to replace him in frontline or lower-value roles while he cultivates more terrain. But eventually, the farm grows beyond the farmer's control. His grasp exceeds his reach. He needs to develop new skills as a manager, planner, and leader. Instead of planting the corn, the farmer must now lead the corn planters.

With growth comes specialization. In addition to planters, the farmer may hire someone to manage his crop and a blacksmith to hammer the plow. He may plant an orchard or acquire a small dairy. But farms—and towns—grow to the limits of their leaders. If he is to progress any further, the farmer must develop the skills to make weighty decisions, balance risk, deal with stress, and lead others on a different plane than ever before. And he must ask himself the ultimate question: "Am I the best person to lead this large company forward?"

The third phase of entrepreneurship transitions the farmer to the Tinker, and leadership is the name of the game. The tinker's development is an internal one: it's building the resilience, focus, and fitness to lead. The tinker must resist the urge to compete and learn to connect. She also needs to step away from the daily delivery of her service.

When the successful business is operating autonomously, the tinker asks, "What's next?" Instead of starting again from scratch, she seeks to bridge other market gaps with her service. The tinker looks for potential overlaps or similar problems, knowing that golden apples sometimes hang from ordinary trees.

This is the Thief phase. With the hard work of innovation complete, the best entrepreneurs learn to connect their ideas with those of others. He might call it "borrowing," but let's be real: no one takes an idea and then gives it back. Noble thieves, like Robin Hood, take what's available and share it with everyone in a new way.

Noble thieves believe in abundance. They believe in mutual profit. They believe in transparency. That's what makes them noble. But it's not what makes them successful.

What will make these founders, farmers, tinkers, and thieves successful is need. It's hunger. They, like the pioneers who founded the four corners of our nation, have real skin in the game, and so do you.

The worldwide economy is changing. Entrepreneurs and spacemen are the only pioneers left. Leave the starry horizon for others. Our time is now.

—CHRIS COOPER

INTRODUCTION

Skin in the game.

That's what I have. The companies I own feed my family.

I am not some arm's-length consultant. I've been an entrepreneur for twenty years. I've started many companies; I sold some, took partners, or went it alone. My education came in the trenches and at the hands of others in countless books, videos, and courses. I've invested hundreds of thousands of dollars in mentorship and been repaid by millions of dollars from mentoring hundreds of other businesses. I learned by doing, by failing, by trying again, by succeeding, by doing it again, and then by teaching.

Now I teach others to do and try again and succeed and do

it again. I show them things they might not have noticed and hold them accountable when they want to put their heads in the sand. I help them make a plan, make a system, make a profit, and make it home in time to catch dinner with their family. I encourage them to *act* instead of *plan,* to move forward instead of spinning their wheels. Occasionally I ask them if it's time to quit.

Theory is nice. Ideas are fun. And the romantic notion of the entrepreneur is an easy sell: tired but happy, driven and passionate, and on track to a guaranteed million-dollar sell-off if she can just survive the grind for three years. Yeah, that's a good one. But theories and ideas don't put food on the table.

What *does* put food on the table? More importantly, what gets the entrepreneur's butt home in time for dinner? What gives him financial security and personal fulfillment? What keeps him going long after the glow of the #hustle has gone out?

The answers to those questions evolve with the four phases of entrepreneurship: founder, farmer, tinker, and thief.

- Is the entrepreneur in the Founder phase? Is she hustling, grinding, thinking every second, and taking rapid action?

- Is she in the Farmer phase? Is she focusing on her primary clients and nurturing her core business?
- Is she a tinker? Is she training herself to be a better leader?
- Or is she a thief? Is she linking her ideas to new ones and leveraging her innovation to serve others more?

A business grows in phases. An entrepreneur must also evolve. The passion that spurs a founder to quit his job, risk his savings, and work seventeen-hour days on a single idea is necessary at startup, but that same passion will probably stop the business from growing later. Instead, the entrepreneur must always be aware that the skills that got him to one level won't be the ones that take him to the next. And his business won't grow until he's developed the skills to advance it.

This book is divided into four parts, each dedicated to a phase of the entrepreneur's evolution from founder to thief, and it will address the most important questions of entrepreneurship:

- What's my revenue goal?
- How much should I be working?
- Where should I focus my work time?
- How should I brand myself?
- What values does my team follow?
- What marketing should my business employ?

- Which "hats" do I wear?
- Who's helping me?
- What type of mentorship should I seek?

And finally,

- What are the primary hurdles to overcome before I move to the next phase?

As your business matures, the answers to these questions will change. The marketing strategies that are most effective for founders are quick and straightforward, but you'll need scalable marketing practices as your business grows. As your audience matures, you'll need to sell your service—first to friends, then to acquaintances once-removed, and finally to strangers. And the same is true for your revenue goals, your branding, and even the values that form the core of your business. Your delivery will go from "me" to "we," and your corporate roles and organizational structure will change. Even the mentorship you require will shift over time.

Every section of this book is relevant to every entrepreneur. But I encourage you to take the *Founder | Farmer | Tinker | Thief* test early (and as often as you like) at Two-Brain.com/test. Your score will help you identify your priorities as you read.

Now, having said that, I don't recommend jumping straight to Part Three to read up on the Tinker phase if that's where your score indicates you to be. Many of the challenges you encounter in the Tinker phase have their roots in the farmer's work. Don't be afraid to take small steps backward before making huge strides forward.

Finally, while this book is meant to define your challenges and solutions clearly, there are really two sides to solving any problem. The first side is determining the best solution; the second is figuring out how to deliver the solution best. Mentorship bridges the two. And no, blog posts and Twitter feeds don't count. I founded a mentorship practice because the internet is full of ideas, unfiltered for advice and unqualified for falsehood. As an entrepreneur, you get to be the hero of your own story. A mentor is your guide. Find one.

PART ONE

—

FOUNDER

"You can have everything in life you want, if you will just help enough other people get what they want."

—ZIG ZIGLAR

Let's begin with the question that matters most: Why?

Why start your own business?

Why you?

Why now?

Maybe you're taking the leap because you have a great idea. Or do you just want to do it YOUR way? Maybe, like me, you feel compelled to carry the ball yourself. Or are you doing it to get rich?

Maybe you're just in love with the idea of entrepreneurship, and the allure of late nights, hair loss, and spiking stress hormones is too magnetic to ignore. Maybe you envision yourself working in a café, wearing "nobody knows I'm a millionaire" jeans, wiping the sawdust from your hand-carved taco-warming bowls off your phone...

Or maybe entrepreneurship is the only thing that will make you happy.

Maybe the promise of seeing your idea become popular thrills you. The opportunity to serve others may fulfill your life's mission. Maybe solving problems will solve YOUR problem. I believe entrepreneurship, done right, can be the path to happiness.

So why are you here?

I'm talking about the big WHY. Your WHY. What is it?

Let's avoid the theoretical realm by applying the coffee-line principle. Pretend I just met you in a coffee line. I see your business name printed on your shirt and ask what you do.

You reply, "I own this company."

"Ah," I say, "What made you decide to open a business?"

What's your response?

Write that down.

We're going to come back to your response a lot over the course of this book. We'll explore it, poke at it, add to it, and infuse it with razor-like clarity.

But first, we're going to talk about two other important words.

THE FOUNDER'S KEYWORD: INNOVATION

You either have an innovative idea, a new approach to an existing idea, or you can expose an untapped market to a great idea. This keyword is an intuitive (dare I say "obvious") one—I doubt you would have launched your company if the market were oversaturated and your idea overdone—but it applies to far more than who your clients are and what you're selling them.

As a founder, you will need to innovate your thinking, your processes, and your systems. It'll be on you to come up with the unique solutions to your unique problems, to figure out how to do $20,000 worth of work on a $2,000 budget. Finding these answers can be tough, but it's essential.

THE FOUNDER'S #HASHTAG

If we were to sum up the Founder phase in a hashtag, it might be #hustle. It could also be #DIY. An entrepreneur in this phase has only one real asset: her time. She's going to be the first one into the shop and the last one out. She'll learn how to fix the broken printer herself. Time is cheap in the Founder phase. Our goal is to get you out of it as quickly as possible.

CORE CONCEPT: ESTABLISH YOUR FOUNDATION

The first exercise I do with every entrepreneur is called "Perfect Day," and that's where we'll start too.

The exercise is a simple one, but I've found that it creates a lot of clarity for my clients. It's a picture of what they want their business to be and, more specifically, how they want their life to look and feel. Your perfect day will serve as your compass on your entrepreneurial journey. So grab your pen, laptop—whatever you like to write with—and let's get to it!

A year from now, when your business is perfect...

What time will you wake up in the morning? Will you start work early or sleep late?

Will you put your kids on the school bus, have a leisurely

coffee, and then cruise to the office, knowing that your early clients were handled just as well as if you'd been there?

Will you go to an office, or do you work from home—or will you go to the beach?

What work will you do within your business? Will you deliver your service or lead others to deliver it?

Will you spend your afternoon further developing the business? Will you take your wife out for lunch? Will you leave early? Will you come back again later?

Some of my clients LOVE to work in their business and prefer to stay hands-on in its daily affairs. Others would like to learn more about the business side and cut back on sewing dresses all day. Both are great. The point is, you have the choice.

Let's keep going. When your business is perfect...

How many vacations will you take each year? Where will you go?

How much net revenue will it take to support this lifestyle?

How much staff do you need, which roles do you need to fill, and how will you support them?

Write it all down with as much detail as you can. (Note: you get bonus points if you put this list somewhere you can see it. When you're having a challenging day, reviewing your "perfect day" will put things in perspective.)

As you can see, the conversation has only just begun. But it's important to start talking about the right things right away. It's too easy to build up a ton of momentum and still be headed in the wrong direction.

Now let's consider what you're willing to sacrifice to reach your perfect day.

THE BRASS RING

Some of the first carnival rides were carousels. You can probably picture them: colorful horses bobbing up and down to organ music, mirrors, and lights glittering in the sun.

On the first carousels, only the inner rows of horses moved. The outer rows were static. So when crowds swarmed the ride, everyone fought for the moving horses.

To entice riders onto the outer rows, enterprising buskers developed a challenge. They hung rings from a pole just beyond the reach of riders on the carousel. Only the passengers on the outer horses could reach the rings, and even then, they could reach the rings only if they stretched to their maximum limit.

Most of the rings were steel, but each carousel had one brass ring. If a rider managed to grab the brass ring, he would win free rides for the day. The brass ring was rare and even harder to reach than its steel counterparts. Many riders fell off, ruining their ride, in their attempt to grab the brass ring. But every carousel ride had a few daredevils willing to risk their turn for the promise of unlimited rides in the future.

Sounds like entrepreneurs to me.

Any brass ring, any rarified prize bestowing benefit to the owner, must necessarily come with risk. Most people are content to wait their turn, enjoy the mild thrill of a moving horse, and then surrender their seat. But a few of us line up with the sole intent of sitting on the edge, stretching ourselves to the max, and risking our ride for a bigger prize. We do so knowing that most rings aren't brass. We know we could fall and that we probably won't be able to afford a second ride. We take our shot without practice beforehand, without help, and with the full knowledge that the carnies don't want us to win.

What makes the ring worth it? Is it the free rides, or is it the risk?

When you define your perfect day, consider the brass ring. How many rides are you willing to gamble before you stop reaching?

What are you willing to give up to get it?

Writing your perfect day will serve as the foundation for your goal-setting process. Defining what you're willing to sacrifice to attain it will help shape your path to achieving it. But there's one more step to consider: the lens through which you view success. What is your bedrock?

TURTLES ALL THE WAY DOWN

In *A Brief History of Time,* Stephen Hawking told the story of a renowned scientist (possibly Bertrand Russell) who gave a public lecture on astronomy:

> He described how the earth orbits around the sun and how the sun, in turn, orbits around the center of a vast collection of stars called our galaxy. At the end of the lecture, a little old lady at the back of the room got up and said: "What you have told us is rubbish. The world is really a flat plate supported on the back of a giant tortoise." The scientist gave a superior smile before replying, "What is the tortoise standing on?" "You're very clever, young man, very clever," said the old lady. "But it's turtles all the way down!"

Knowledge—in science, in myth, and in your business—requires a foundation of absolute truth.

If I ask your staff, "Why do you open at 9 a.m.?" are they likely to say, "Because that's the time we've always opened"?

If so, what answer would they give if I ask, "Why have you always opened at that time?"

Would they say, "Well, that's what time everyone opens on this street"?

And if I asked, "Why does everyone on this street open at nine a.m.?" What answer would I get then? It's turtles all the way down.

But if your staff answered the first question with, "We polled our best clients, and they prefer to start visiting at 9 a.m." or, "Traffic patterns on this block show that people arrive around 9:30 a.m.," then I would know that your business had a solid foundation of data.

When I worked in a treadmill store years ago, a traveling sales rep subjected me to such questions.

"Why do you open Monday to Friday from nine until five,

then open for a half-day on Saturday and stay closed all day on Sunday?"

My answer: "Because that's when people come in."

He asked, "What other times have you tried?"

I backpedaled: "Well, no one else in this minimall is open on Sunday. We'd be the only one."

He continued, "Why do they all close on Sundays?"

Finally, exasperated, I answered, "Well, I'm not going to work seven days a week! I need my Saturday afternoons and Sundays off!"

His point was that most people don't buy treadmills between nine in the morning and five in the evening because they're at work. They buy treadmills between 5 p.m. and 9 p.m. and on the weekends because that's when they're free to shop. So why not run wide open for two weeks, track when people want to visit most, and then close for the rest of the time?

As he asked me those questions, I realized I had no bedrock. I didn't have *real* reasons for doing things the way I did. It was turtles all the way down. My business was a house of cards, and each card was just a guess.

Here's how we build foundations at Two-Brain Business, my mentoring practice:

1. We start with your values. What's your personal, nonnegotiable bedrock? What are you not willing to sacrifice to uphold them? For example, I believe in transparency and fairness, so I don't offer discounts at my gym.
2. Next, we build a playbook so that your staff will find it easy to do things the way you want them done. They don't have to guess what the owner wants from them. The playbook becomes *their* bedrock.
3. Finally, we examine the gold standards in your industry and ask, "What are the best doing? What's a ten out of ten?" and work to improve all of it.

Just as you can't add weight to a house of cards, you can't grow a business without a strong foundation.

When a business owner books a consultation call with me, I spend the first ten minutes asking questions. I want to know their story. I want to see if I can help them. And I want to find their bedrock.

So I ask about their perfect day. I ask them to tell me the story of their business. I ask, "Who's helping you with this?" But what I'm really trying to find is their foundation: the systems on which their business runs. When I discover a lack of systems, I want to know their goals. And if they can't clearly state their goals—their giant, big WHY IN THE SKY—then I ask about their values.

THE FOUNDER'S VALUES

Company values in the Founder phase are the founder's own. The business exists to serve the founder, not itself, and the products, services, pricing, and first clients are all determined by the founder's preferences and experiences. For better or worse, the founder will lean heavily on her own preferences (and budget) when deciding what to sell and what to charge for it.

Later, these values will be redefined to leverage the education and experience of the team. But for now, the founder should start by defining where the business is going and then clearly recording the unimpeachable values that will carry them there.

Most of us live out our values every day but never take the time to define them. That's about to change. Here's a values exercise we use with our founder clients.

Name five positive influencers in your life. What's the biggest lesson they taught you? Take the time to record their names, qualities, and the specific lessons you took from them. Now, beneath each of the five, go back and write instructions to yourself—and your staff—on how to deliver these values to your clients. For example:

> "My grandfather taught me to work hard, not fast."

> "We value consistency of effort instead of intensity. It's more important to come back tomorrow than to push beyond safe limits."

Next, record five negative influencers in your life. Think of fake friends, bad bosses, or ineffective teachers. What did they teach you NOT to do? Take the time to record specific names and lessons. Now, beneath each of those five, write instructions to yourself (and your staff) on things to avoid. What will you never do in this company? Here's one of mine.

One of my first employers told me, "Do as I say, not as I do." His message made me think of him as a hypocrite, and I questioned everything he told me.

> "We practice the motto 'do what you say you will do' because we believe in making only commitments and rules that we can keep ourselves. We don't overpromise and underdeliver, and we only ask staff to do things we're willing to do ourselves."

With that, you have the first iteration of your company playbook, founded on the bedrock of your core values.

CORE CONCEPT: THE KINGMAKER EQUATION

Business success must be reduced to its core elements before it can be measured. The intangibles—helping our clients, saving lives, making them feel gorgeous—these are the elements of our jobs, not our businesses. I'll wait for someone else to make "good haircuts" measurable, observable, and repeatable in more than an empirical form. My job is to make entrepreneurs profitable. And that means starting with a simple definition of success.

Your idea of success will be different from mine. After twenty-two years of coaching fitness, I'm no longer jumping for joy at the prospect of teaching burpees at 5 a.m. But we can all agree that financial success is measured by profit, and lifestyle success is measured by the freedom to choose how we spend our time.

The two measurable variables of success (financial and lifestyle) are profit and time.

With those two variables in mind, the master equation—I call it the "Kingmaker"—for success in any business is:

$$\frac{\$}{T}$$

$ (Profit) over T (Time)

Let's consider three sample cases. Each of these was taken from a recent call with a client at Two-Brain Business:

- Case #1: $1,000,000 gross revenue; 10% profit margin; 12-hour workday (plus Saturday)
- Case #2: $600,000 gross revenue; 25% profit margin; 12-hour workday (weekends off)
- Case #3: $300,000 gross revenue; 40% profit margin; 3-hour workweek (yes, work*week*)

Which is the better business?

CASE #1: ($1,000,000 GROSS, 10% PROFIT MARGIN, 66 HOURS PER WEEK)

$ = $100,000 per year (net revenue)

÷ 66 hours/week

= $29 per hour

CASE #2: $600,000 GROSS REVENUE; 25% PROFIT MARGIN; 12-HOUR WORKDAY (WEEKENDS OFF)

$ = $150,000 per year (net revenue)

÷ 60 hours/week

= $48.07 per hour

CASE #3: $300,000 GROSS REVENUE; 40% PROFIT MARGIN; 3-HOUR WORKWEEK

$ = $120,000

÷ 3 hours/week

= $769.23 per hour

Obviously, the third case is the best business. But is that optimal for YOU?

Do you want a job working in your business, or do you want to do other things with your time?

If you want to be an entrepreneur, #3 is obviously best because you can leverage your time to build the *next* business. I did this with Ignite, then Spark (which I later sold), then Two-Brain Business, and now the Two-Brain Workshop. There are more companies coming because I have time to work on them.

If you just want to do "the job," Case #3 is still best because you can work as much as you want to but aren't required to work. Your job as a business owner will entail doing the things a business owner does, and you can't do those things while you're out on the floor. But when those things are done...go make shoes, glaze the donuts, or paint nails!

It's worth noting again: I calculated profit, not gross revenue, because gross really doesn't matter in the service industry. $100,000 gross on a remote training business without overhead is far better than $100,000 gross in a brick-and-mortar location. And $1,000,000 gross isn't impressive at all if there's no profit: the business owner has just built a huge leaky bucket.

Also worth noting: in the first two examples, the owners have really bought themselves a reasonably high-paying job. Twenty-nine dollars per hour is marginally better than most would make as, say, a personal trainer. The problem is that their time as an owner is worth far more.

Leveling up to being paid what you're worth requires

math and mentorship. First, you need a clear picture of what your time is actually worth, as judged by a neutral third party. And second, you need a clear path toward higher value for your time.

You should be a millionaire if that's what you want. You deserve it. But millionaires don't spend time sweeping floors because they know their denominator—time—is finite. Start increasing the numerator—profit—but don't sacrifice your life to do it.

THE FOUNDER'S INCOME GOAL

Your income goal in the Founder phase is what we call "breakeven plus." It's also to develop the habit of paying yourself.

The point of business ownership is to get paid by your business, but many owners fall into the trap of reinvesting every single cent they make back into the business. Their strategy is noble in theory, but in practice, it creates the wrong behavior.

Most entrepreneurs understand that they won't make a profit in the first week. They spend everything they make on growing the business: they hire staff, upgrade equipment, or boost their marketing budget. They plan to take a paycheck at some undetermined point in the future but, for now, they're willing to delay short-term gratification for a longer-term gain.

What these selfless entrepreneurs—and you—may not realize is that your expenses will always expand to fill your revenues. There's always somewhere else to spend the money. So before long, the founder's business is making more money, but she is still keeping none of it.

PAY YOURSELF FIRST

David fixes computer networks. He has a few clients: businesses just large enough to need their own server, local hotels that share a reservation system, and accounting firms that need to share client data.

When David launched as a solopreneur, he was setting up networks himself. He'd buy the necessary parts with his credit card and pay it off when a client paid him for his work. At night, he took courses online to learn how to work with more extensive networks. He set his rates by taking what others charged in larger cities and subtracting a few percent to fit his smaller city's market.

After a few months, David noticed that many of his clients required similar parts: routers, Ethernet cables, and mounting brackets. He decided to purchase more of these parts in advance and hold them in inventory to speed up his delivery time. He didn't want to put the parts on a credit card, so he spent three months' profit and emptied his bank account to buy the parts because he knew he could sell them at a markup.

Instead of a one-off, David's reinvestment approach became a habit. His money flowed back into his business, paying off his equipment and education, buying new parts, and paying for new courses.

After a year, David spotted an opportunity: he could buy space in a large, secure server on the West Coast and then rent it out to his smaller clients who couldn't afford their own. So he committed to the monthly fee—another "investment" in his company—and a few clients took him up on the offer. David still wasn't paying himself, but he wasn't losing money either. Without anyone to compare himself against, he figured his business was running about average.

Then the local school board asked him for a quote to service their systems for a year. It would be the most significant job David had ever done. He'd need to hire someone else or dedicate himself to the school board almost full time for a few months. The job would eat up his time, but it would also pay him the most. David decided to go for it.

When he got the job, David was ecstatic. He'd never seen

a five-digit number on a check before. But before the first payment arrived, he had to upgrade his equipment. So he borrowed from his retirement plan to buy new diagnostic software and hire an assistant. The first check from the school board went to equipment purchases and his new staff.

Then he realized the new staff member wasn't familiar with the software used by the school board, so he had to pay for training. And new tools. And transportation. And lunch.

When David's first tax bill hit, he was running a $300,000-per-year company, had nothing in the bank, and wasn't paying himself a dime. That's when he called Two-Brain Business.

"Everyone is making money except me," he said. "My suppliers, my server hosts, my staff, and the freaking government!"

He continued, "I'd make more money if I'd just taken a part-time job with the school board and done the work myself! But now I own a pretty successful company. I can't just shut down and take a job."

David's choice to forego a personal wage sounds noble: he's willing to starve a little today to earn a larger payout tomorrow. Here's the thing, though: he's actually taking the easy way out. He's martyring himself and his family. And a business that doesn't pay its owner is not a successful business.

I was lucky enough to dodge this bullet. When I opened my first business, I had no cash reserve. There was no buffer to carry me through the first few months. I had to get paid on the first Friday, and every Friday after that, or my family wouldn't have grocery money.

I opened on a Monday. When clients came in to buy their personal training sessions, it was easy to say, "Just pay me next week. It's no problem." I guess I thought I was building rapport.

On Tuesday, it got a bit harder to defer payment. I only had three days left to earn the $900 I needed to make that week. My credit card terminal wasn't installed, but when a client said, "No problem, I'll just pay next week," I stepped forward and said, "I can take a check."

On Wednesday, I was way past allowing a client to leave without paying. And by Thursday, I was desperate. I started asking clients to buy large packages of sessions in advance because my Friday deadline was looming. The hurdle of asking for money was still in place, but necessity vaulted me over it. I nearly emptied the business's bank account, but I paid myself on time because I had to.

If I didn't need the money on Friday, I probably wouldn't have gotten it. I wouldn't have asked clients to pay in advance, or worse, I would have spent the money on new equipment or an ad to draw in more clients and fallen into the trap of reinvestment. The pressure I felt as each day passed honed my focus. Our brains are wired for urgency: we do the things that are urgent but not necessarily the things that are important. However, we can leverage this urgency to do the important things.

So pay yourself first. Calculate the minimum amount you need to live, cutting as many expenses as possible but no more. Break that number down into a weekly amount. Then write your first fifty-two checks to yourself: post-date them for every Friday for the next year. Put them in an envelope and take them to the bank. Now you're committed: you've created your first positive constraint.

When we started teaching this strategy to our mentoring clients, two purchased houses in the first month. They didn't miraculously start making an extra $700 per month; they merely changed their spending priorities. Little purchases—things they were buying without paying much attention—were adding up to more than a mortgage payment in both cases. Paying themselves first made a big impact.

If you don't absolutely need the money, develop the practice anyway: write checks for $100 to yourself for the first three months. Postdate them for each Friday, and deposit them.

Paying yourself requires discipline. It's a mindset as much as a practice.

In the Farmer phase, your income strategy will be "Profit First." But in the Founder phase, it's "Pay Yourself First." As soon as your cash flow (your monthly revenue minus your monthly expenses) reaches breakeven, pay yourself something before you buy anything else.

CORE CONCEPT: THE VALUE OF YOUR TIME

This is one of my favorite pictures. A friend of mine in Haslet, Texas, sent me this picture after earning his CEO mug. The CEO mug is a reward I give business owners after they graduate from my Incubator program. It's a bright yellow badge of honor. Someday you might earn one too.

What I love most about the picture is the homemade contraption under which the mug is placed.

At coffee shops around the world, you can order a "pour-over" coffee. A great pour-over starts with great beans, freshly ground. Then the barista heats the water to volcanic temperatures and slowly pours it through the grinds in a clockwise motion. Instead of flowing straight down through the middle of a filter, every drop of water touches fresh grounds, making for a much richer cup. It's worth the wait. You can buy pour-over machines, but they're not cheap.

Jonathan didn't have time to sit over a coffee pot, and he couldn't afford a pour-over machine, so he built one himself. It's a simple DIY project, and the outcome is a fantastic cup of coffee.

When you're launching your business, you'll have to decide where your time is best spent. On your first day as an entrepreneur, you do every little task yourself to save money, and that's fine. You don't have any money yet, and frankly, your time isn't worth much. But I want you to think a few months ahead, and plan to break free from the DIY mindset typical to founders.

There's no shortage of media content online about "lean startups" and "putting in the work" and, my favorite, "grinding." These are usually the mottos of struggling entrepreneurs. They don't know what to do, so they just do all of it. Or they avoid the problematic hard work by doing everything else instead.

In *The War of Art*, Steven Pressfield writes about "the resistance," a mysterious force that stops you from doing the real work. Resistance comes in many forms—procrastination, distraction, multitasking—and you're going to run into it at some point.

It will be very tempting to assemble a new desk instead of picking up the phone to cold-call a doctor's office. You'll want to install your own flooring instead of inviting another therapist out to lunch. Or you'll want to spend twenty-five minutes making a cup of coffee. You'll tell yourself you're saving money or embracing "the hustle." This is the trap of DIY: work will always expand to fill the time and space you give it.

In the first week of your new business, you should be

walking into doctors' offices with sandwiches and referral pads. You should NOT be painting the walls of your clinic, but you will be tempted to do that work instead of the hard stuff that only you can do. It's a trap. Your key asset, the one thing that you can leverage to build a successful company and the real measuring stick isn't money; it's time. You open a business to earn a higher return on your time, not to buy yourself a job.

Soon, your time will be far too valuable to spend on DIY projects. Hire someone out, and then find work that will cover the cost. Here's how to do it.

CALCULATE YOUR EHR (EFFECTIVE HOURLY RATE)

One of my business mentors, Dan Martell, uses a formula he calls "Effective Hourly Rate" to determine where an entrepreneur should be spending his time:

> Every entrepreneur has a thing I call the EHR. Your Effective Hourly Rate. The easiest way to get to that is just to take the gross revenue in your business and divide it by 2,000. That's about the hours that you work in a year. Figuring 100,000 in revenue divided by 2,000, that's $50 an hour. Once you know your EHR, and if you're doing a million, it's 5,000 an hour. There are real numbers involved.

Martell's formula has value because every task you perform can be held up against this standard:

> Once I know my EHR, I make a list of all the activities that I work on a weekly and biweekly basis, then I rank-order them based on the cost it would take for me to get somebody else to support me in that role. If it doesn't touch the customer, that's another good filter. If it touches the customer, you want to hold on to that for a bit.

It's the secret to entrepreneurship that Michael Gerber and John C. Maxwell and dozens of others write about: moving from "doing the job" to "owning the business." You don't need to hire a full-time employee to free up time. You can move from role to role incrementally.

Keep in mind:

- You must replace yourself in each role *completely*. That means identifying the tasks to be done, codifying those tasks, setting a "gold standard" for each, and then evaluating success.
- You must have a clear plan for the higher-value work you'll do. Otherwise, you'll be sucked back into minutiae.
- Finally, even if you DON'T have a great idea right now, you need to be ready for the next one. A huge reason why my companies grow so fast is that I don't

have a permanent role in any of them. I can replace myself quickly when a new opportunity comes along.

So take the time to calculate your EHR. Do it now. The answer might be scary—it might even be tempting to go find a minimum-wage job instead of plugging away at your business—but we need to know this number so we can build on it.

THE FOUNDER'S TIME GOAL

I've never met a business owner who *didn't* have a great idea.

I've done over two thousand free calls with entrepreneurs who need help. And almost every time, I hear this:

> "I really want to get my X started, but I'm too busy."

Or,

> "I listen to your podcast and I'm intrigued by your Z, but I don't have the staff to help me run it."

Or,

> "I can't afford to pay my staff to start a Y program. I can barely get them to clean the pool deck at night after closing time!"

A lack of ideas is almost never the problem. The problem is nearly always a lack of action, and it's a solvable one.

MOVING TO HIGHER-VALUE ROLES

Every business owner wears several different hats over the course of the day. We call each of these hats "roles," and the activities done while wearing the hats are "tasks." And your job as a founder is to assign a dollar amount to each one.

How do we get there?

Start by recording every role in your business. Here are some samples:

- Salon manager
- Hairdresser
- Bookkeeper
- Marketer
- Cleaner

Each of these roles is distinct from the others, and the odds are high that someone else will do a better job at them than you will. They'll care about it more, and if you hand responsibility over to them, you will have more time to pursue your passion: coaching. Or tailoring. Or marketing. Or drinking coffee with your feet on your desk.

Don't assign anyone to each role yet. Your own name might even appear next to every role at first. Resist the urge to mold the roles to fit the people working for your company (even if you're a solopreneur). The people should fit the roles, not vice versa.

Next, measure and record how much time is necessary to complete each role every week. Parkinson's Law says that work will expand to fill the time you give it. If it takes you five hours per week to clean, but your staff needs ten hours to do the same job, you'll always be tempted to jump back in and do it yourself. Avoid that temptation by giving your staff time lines to complete each task.

Use your EHR to determine the "replacement value" of each role. What would it cost to replace you? Can a sixteen-year-old do a better job on social media than you currently are? What's that role worth?

Then replace yourself in one role. This is a prerequisite to reach Farmer phase: you must buy yourself the time to work on your business instead of in your business. Hire someone else to fulfill the least expensive role. Use that time to work on a higher-value role, like marketing or sales.

Finally, monitor, track, and evaluate. How closely

does the staff person adhere to your checklist, template, or instructions? After three months, evaluate their progress. If they're doing well, enjoying their work, and the net revenue created by handing off the position is greater than their pay, you've won: keep going.

The hard part is backing off and allowing the staff member to learn the role. It's tough to pull away. However, a good entrepreneur isn't measured by her time investment; a good entrepreneur can replace herself in her business.

And move up the ladder to the next role.

Every business has a skill hierarchy. Some roles will simply require a different level of passion and expertise. Some, like "cleaner," are easy to shift to someone else. As you move up the hierarchy toward higher-skill roles, the time required to shift responsibility increases, but you'll move closer to your perfect day by large leaps, not small steps.

For example, there's a great chance you're not the best cleaner in your business. Who is? What's a cleaner paid in your area? For me, $15 per hour is a fair rate for a good cleaner.

If I pay a cleaner for an hour each weeknight, then that's $75 per week, or about $300 per month. But if I commit to using my "cleaning" time to a higher-value role, I can produce far more than $300 in new revenue for my business.

Hiring a cleaner, in my case, creates twenty hours per month. I can use that time for marketing, developing new programs, improving our continuing education program, creating content, building a marketing funnel, meeting with clients—or sleeping. Tucking my kids into bed. Eating dinner with my wife.

The rule I make for mentoring clients is this: hire the cleaner on a three-month contract. While they're working, move on to the next role until you've produced the revenue to pay the cleaner. Then go home.

After three months, evaluate your cleaner on a 1-to-10 scale on each item in their tasks checklist. Are they reaching 9 or above in all categories? Do they like the work? Are you using the time for CEO work? If yes to all the above, extend the contract and move to the NEXT role.

In each case, you're working to replace yourself in a lower-value role to make time for higher-value roles.

Now, to be clear: low-value roles are filled with high-value people. The "low-value" title refers to the role's potential to grow your business. A filthy bathroom might limit your growth, but cleaning the bathroom yourself won't bring you closer to wealth. The best option is to move responsibility to someone else and leverage the time saved.

If you are not yet in the financial position to hire someone else for three months, that's okay! But what about an hour? Can you afford to delegate (or eliminate) the lowest-value hour of your day?

To determine the lowest-value hour of your time, pull out your list of Roles and Tasks. Assign a value to each role if you haven't already. (Remember, this is the cost to replace you in that role.)

Next, do a time valuation: wear a watch for a week and record every role in which you spend more than five minutes. (This is tedious, I know, but there are apps that can help.) If you spend more than five minutes on your email, write that down. Think of it as a food journal for entrepreneurship.

Then identify the lowest-value hour of your day. Many gym owners are surprised to discover their lowest-value hour is one in which they're teaching a class. Many dentists realize their assistants can easily replace them in most procedures. Whatever (and whenever) it is, "buy" yourself that hour. Pay someone else to take your evening class. Pay an administrator to answer your emails or update your social media. Commit to free up that hour for three months and schedule a reminder to measure the revenue gained at the end of that term.

Finally, use the new hour to work on higher-value roles, like sales. Or build a staff-training program. Or start your nutritionist team, launch your kids' program, or build brand awareness. No matter what you choose, build these new programs with a plan to transition them to someone else.

THE FOUNDER'S BRAND

In the Founder phase, the entrepreneur is her own brand. She might call her café "The Soultown Grill," but her first customers will come to Mary's place because they want to eat Mary's food and talk to Mary while she serves them.

The founder's largest challenge is usually awareness: people probably don't know The Soultown Grill exists. But who does know? Mary's friends and family. They'll be her first clients. They'll want to help her because they care about her.

The founder's personal brand and business brand are synonymous at this stage. This will change later, but for now, the entrepreneur's friends and family *should* be her first clients. Even if Mary's a lousy cook, they should support her (and they should pay full price and tip very well too.)

We'll discuss marketing strategy shortly, but the key to remember here is that the founder's first clients will have a personal connection. Advertising won't attract them. They'll be drawn in because of their relationship to you. And you should use those relationships to build your business and brand awareness.

Many entrepreneurs are too modest about their goals. Maybe they're embarrassed to take the leap in front of their friends. Maybe they don't want to "impose" on their relationships. So they downplay their new business in conversation. They fail to overtly invite their friends and neighbors. They don't bring their venture up at the dinner table. Maybe they've been taught it's impolite to ask for money and feel as if inviting those they care about is the same thing. It's not.

We all opened our businesses to serve others, to solve their problems. We can probably solve their problems better than anyone else. Why don't we want to solve our family's problems first?

Why wouldn't your mother be your first nutrition client?

Why wouldn't you want your dad to buy his suit from you?

Why wouldn't you offer to do your pastor's taxes?

Why wouldn't your best friend come to you to have her teeth cleaned?

No one will care for them like you will. No one will give them better value for their money, and yes, you'll charge them the same rate as everyone else.

One of my first business mentors was a mechanic named Nick. We were friends, and I used to sit in his dining room in the late evening and complain about my business.

He told me, "You need to raise your prices."

I would always counter with, "Nick, all these people are my friends! I can't do that to my friends!"

And he'd always say, "If they're your friends, they'll pay anything you ask them to."

One night, he forced the issue. He wrote me a check for his gym membership that was 10 percent higher than what he currently paid. It was 10 percent higher than my highest rate.

"There," he said. "That's your new price. If you charge anyone less than what I just paid, you're screwing me— your friend. Now go raise your rates to this new amount."

I did. Some people quit. To them, ten bucks per month was more important than our imaginary "friendship." But the people who really cared stayed. And as I started talking about my gym business to people at family parties, they all wanted to join. They knew I'd take better care of them than anyone because I cared. And none of them ever complained about price or expected a special deal.

As a new entrepreneur, you don't have much to build your brand. But you have your reputation and your relationships. Use them.

CORE CONCEPT: AFFINITY MARKETING

Where do your clients come from? The best clients come from personal connection to your brand. The next-best clients come from a personal relationship with your clients.

An Affinity Marketing plan looks like a bull's-eye. In the Founder phase, the personal connections used to grow a business are the entrepreneur's own. The founder is at the center of the business's first Affinity Marketing bull's-eye. Each ring or "loop" represents a new audience for your service. As we radiate out from the center, your audience size increases, but their affinity decreases. As we move from the center toward the outer rings, audience awareness cools off. You'll have to do more work to "warm up" a potential client to get them to purchase, and even more work to keep them. The further from the center you get, the more education a prospective client will require before signing up for your service or buying anything from you.

Starting from the middle dot and working outward, here are the "Affinity Loops":

- **Axial Loop**—Your best clients (or, if you don't have any clients yet, you). It's the center dot in our target, the people on whom the entire business pivots.
- **Affection Loop**—The people closest to your best clients. Their spouse, parents, or kids.
- **Activity Loop**—The people who work with your best clients (or your own coworkers). This loop could also contain complementary service professionals. For example, if you're a personal trainer, your "occupational loop" could include nutritionists or physical therapists. These are people with whom your best clients share an activity. It might also be a recreational activity, like midnight basketball.
- **Acquaintance Loop**—The "friends of friends," the people with whom you have one degree of separation. You might not know them directly, but you share a friend in common. And they, in turn, share similar characteristics to your best clients. For example, your best clients might golf at the local country club. Other

golfers at the same club are in the Acquaintance Loop of your best clients, even if they aren't already friends.

- **Attention Loop**—Future (or past) clients who aren't currently using your service but are still active on your email list or another conversation, like a business owners' group. They're not paying you money, but they're still paying attention.

- **Awareness Loop**—People in your neighborhood or in a similar niche who are aware of you but aren't exactly sure what you offer or how your service works. They probably don't know anyone actively using your service.

- **Audiences Loop**—Those in your target niche who aren't yet aware of your service or how you can help them.

- **Ambient Loop**—Every potential client for your service who isn't disqualified or "filtered out." If you perform surgery in Idaho, the people in your Ambient Loop would include anyone who would drive to your location for surgery, can afford the surgery, need the surgery, or know someone who does.

The first four affinity loops are where we'll focus our attention in the Founder phase.

CHEAT SHEET

CLIENT	Axial Loop	Affection Loop	Activity Loop	Acquaintance Loop	Attention Loop	Awareness Loop	Audiences Loop

www.**twobrain**.com

THE FOUNDER'S MARKETING PLAN

Affinity Marketing in the Founder stage is pretty straight-forward: concentrate your efforts on your axial, affection, activity, and acquaintance loops.

Before you start drawing them in, though, it's essential to work through a client's interaction with your business. You need to anticipate every step they will take—from awareness to interest to purchase and beyond—so your clients don't fall through gaps in your service.

MAPPING YOUR CLIENT JOURNEY

There's a big difference between a hairdresser's salon and a haircut joint in the mall. The first relies on repeat business from clients who visit for years; the second relies on one-time drop-ins from people seeking cheap, quick, and convenient service. With expensive mall rent and overhead, most founders will start in a small salon with a few clients and an appointment book.

The salon owner-founder must take great care to avoid the business model of the mall clip joint. She must cultivate relationships with future clients herself, maintain those clients on a predictable schedule, and keep them for years. She doesn't have time to wait for new clients to find her, and she can't afford to wait for them to decide when they need a haircut.

When she maps her client journey, she identifies how long a client should wait between visits and creates a process for making new appointments (and following up with clients who are overdue for a trim). She determines what action she'll take when a client doesn't arrive on time and what to do on their birthdays. She'll note when clients typically want an extra service—for example, ladies getting their toenails painted before beach season—and plan her schedule around her clients' future needs.

This practice will serve the client best. But it will also avoid randomness in the founder's marketing and sales plan. If she knows that the average man needs his hair cut every six weeks, she can plan her cash flow around that calendar. She can say to her male clients, "Let's book our next appointment for six weeks from today," as they're paying for their current appointment, instead of waiting for them to (maybe) call her later.

Client retention *is* sales. Booking appointments *is* marketing. The person most likely to buy from you next is the client buying from you now. With that in mind, let's map your client journey.

If you own a hairdressing business, your client's story goes like this.

A client thinks, "I need a new hairstyle."

She enters your shop because it looks like she can get something new. You ask what she'd like and then point her toward the best look for her. You're the mentor: her Yoda.

As your staff cuts her hair, you notice the anxiety on her face: Will this backfire? Will she look worse than before? Will she hate the new cut? That anxiety is mixed with excitement. The client might love the new haircut. Her friends might compliment her on it. Men might find her more attractive.

Then, the big reveal: it looks fantastic! She happily leaves a big tip and ventures back out into the world.

But THEN what happens? When does she come back?

When will you speak next? When will she pay you for more of your excellent service?

Mapping your client's experience is one of the first steps to growing your business. This exercise will tell you:

- Where your ideal clients come from
- What their first impression of your brand must be
- What their first visit should include and how long it will take
- What happens immediately after their first visit
- How their second visit is planned and scheduled
- How long a client stays with your company

The client's journey will describe your sales process and your retention strategy. In the Founder phase, the only metrics you'll track will be ARM, LEG, and profit. Mapping out the client journey will show you how to increase each of them. (We'll tackle those in a moment.)

Your exercise: start with the first point of contact with a new client. How do they book an appointment? What questions do you ask, and what are the options presented to them? How do you take payment for your service, and how do you schedule a follow-up? How long should they wait before returning? What emails or communication will follow your conversation? How will your staff support it? What will keep your clients coming back?

For example, we teach entrepreneurs in the fitness industry to use a prescriptive model.

The first visit is a consultation, with many questions asked of the potential client. After a few minutes, the coach or salesperson makes a "prescription": a few days of exercise, plus a nutrition plan. They stick to the core offerings of the business. They also give the client a few options for delivery: Does she prefer to exercise one-on-one or in a group? At home or in the gym? The client then chooses an option based on her preferences. The coach accepts payment and moves on to scheduling the rest of the client's journey.

First, he books the client's first personal training appointment. Next, he adds the client to an automated email list, which sends the client educational videos and "homework" on the days she doesn't attend the gym. Finally, the coach schedules the next appointment for follow-up. This is key to retention in the service industry.

Here's a sample client journey a gym owner might use:

CLIENT JOURNEY

Two-Brain Business

1ST MEETING	1ST WORKOUT	2ND	3RD	4TH	5TH	GOAL REVIEW
No-Sweat Intro	Private 1:1				PRIVATE 1:1	Goal Review
In-Body Scan	Basic fitness test				WOD	InBody or nutrition checklist
Register For Onramp	Score on BFT, book second appointment				Ask For Preference, 1:1 or Group. Book Goal Review	Choose package
Welcome package	First workout badge				Onramp Graduation certificate, picture on the internet	Welcome to the Tribe package
Email, invite to SugarWOD, private FB group, describe what happens next, trigger onboarding automation	Intro to nutrition video, intro in FB group, check addition on SugarWOD, fistbumps				Goal review automation, letter to self, perfect day exercise, congratulations in FB group, postcard	Catalyst code doc, nutrition modules, addition on Strava, bike loan
Sales, Joy Girl	Coach				JoyGirl, Coach	Sales

The document will work for any business as long as it includes the following six criteria:

- **Activity**—What's the client doing at this stage?
- **Measurement**—How will we measure success at this stage?
- **Outcome**—What's the desired result of this stage?
- **Reward**—How will we encourage the client to continue to the next stage?
- **Follow-up**—What will the client receive between in-person appointments or meetings?
- **Staff**—Who will carry out the various duties in this stage?

Mapping the client's journey sets the stage for long-term retention. But it also makes "selling" easier for the owner and coach.

CORE CONCEPT: ARM AND LEG

When we teach metrics to business owners, we keep it simple: ARM and LEG. Your ARM (average revenue per client per month) is a measure of sales and marketing, and LEG (length of engagement) is a measure of your operations. And a client's lifetime value to your business is the product of ARM times LEG:

ARM × LEG = the lifetime value of the customer

So, for example, if you charge $200 per month (that's your ARM), and keep a client for one month (your LEG), then your marketing efforts were worth $200.

If you keep that same client for two visits, your efforts were worth $400.

Keep that same client for a year, and your efforts were worth $2,400.

If you keep them for ten years, your efforts were worth $24,000.

And the cost to acquire them is the same in every case.

We work VERY hard on sales and marketing, but fortune is found in retention, and good retention isn't just about birthday cards and automated emails. Good retention is about systems. Your ARM and LEG are multipliers of each other. Amazing operations with no sales? You're multiplying by zero. Great marketing with low prices and poor retention? Zero. You need both to be strong, and we'll be discussing different strategies for each stage of your entrepreneurial development.

The simplest way to increase your ARM is to charge more for the same services. Many entrepreneurs are terrified of raising their rates, but there are other ways to boost your ARM if a rate hike makes you nervous.

You can prescribe additional visits or services. (In the Farmer phase, you'll read about the "prescriptive model," which shifts the perspective of an entrepreneur from an "order taker" to a "trusted advisor.") Or you can increase the total value of each transaction with complementary services or add-ons.

I recently witnessed a perfect example in one of my regular lunchtime spots. It was a cold, rainy day, and two construction workers came in and stood in line behind me. Both planned to order sandwiches and coffee to go and then eat in the truck with the heater blaring.

But the hostess approached them and said, "You guys look drenched. Go sit down, and I'll bring you coffee. You don't have to stand in line and wait. Here, give me your coats."

So they sat down. A few minutes later, she brought them hot coffee. "I bet you guys could use some soup. We've got a pretty hearty beef stew today. How's that sound?"

One of the workers said, "That sounds pretty f***ing great."

The other guy laughed and said, "Yeah, it does."

Then the waitress said, "I've got these really great cheese buns. Why don't I warm them up a bit and butter them for you? Then I'll grab your soup and sandwiches."

How could they say no?

Their bill was close to double what they anticipated spending. But both of them loved it. When they left, the first worker said, "See ya Monday. We're going to bring the whole crew!"

And the other worker said, "Like hell we are. Let them figure it out for themselves!" They laughed, left a big tip, and went back out into the rain. It was a win-win-win-win: a win for them (full belly, warm meal), a win for the waitress (big tip), a victory for the café owner (double their bill), and a win for me because I want to see that café succeed. I eat at least two of my meals there every day. I want it to be around for the next thirty years!

You can improve your ARM by charging more for your services (increasing your rates), increasing the frequency of your service to the client (they visit more often), and upping the value of the transaction with complementary services or add-ons. Improving your LEG means perfecting your operations, and I'll get you started on that piece right now:

1. Complete your Roles and Tasks exercise, if you haven't already.
2. Write a clear definition of success in each role. The ultimate measure of success is increased LEG.
3. Consider the gold standards in your industry and map a path to match them. What are the best businesses like yours in the world doing?
4. Map the client journey. What happens, and when? Who's responsible for making sure?
5. Set up automated checkpoints (flags, emails, actions, rewards, badging) along the client journey. Ten-year client anniversary gifts and birthday cards are great ideas but really irrelevant without a system for consistency. Imagine sending half your clients a birthday card or text and not the other half.
6. Track your LEG every single month. If your retention score is low, you'll know you have an operational problem.

Every one of us thinks our business is nearly perfect. We believe that our systems are amazing, that our clients "get us," and that we're building some kind of emotional bank account with them. We're blind to operational problems because we think our kid is the most handsome in school: "Every girl should love you, schmoopy! You're mommy's handsome boy!" That's why we need objective data, like ARM and LEG. And we need to track it over time to see the impact of our changes. The same goes for all of your latest and greatest ideas. Is your new idea having any real effect? Unless you're measuring LEG over time, you don't know.

Objective measurements like ARM and LEG help you push past personal bias from your business and give you clarity. Sales are fun, but (*don't do it, Chris*) without retention (*resist!*), you won't have (*he's gonna do it*) a LEG to stand on. (*Groan.*)

SALES IN THE FOUNDER STAGE

One of the largest myths in sales and marketing is that "you have to get your name out there." While it's important for clients to be able to find you, just hanging a sign isn't enough to bring them through the door.

Your first sales goal is to increase the ARM of the clients you already have. How else can you serve those who are already paying you? What other problems can you solve for them? How else can you improve their lives?

Your second sales goal is to increase your LEG. It's far easier to keep a good client than to find a new one. And the longer a client stays with your business, the more valuable he or she becomes.

Your third sales goal is to reach the people who surround

your best clients. I'll walk you through our preferred strategy for selling to this group—called the Attention Loop of Affinity Marketing—in the Farmer section.

Remember, you can't be a successful business owner without selling your service. Personally, I hate feeling like a salesman. Maybe you don't. Either way, when you're writing your Roles and Tasks document, mark a special place for the person in charge of sales.

Now, here's the thing: if selling is "everyone's job," it's no one's job. And yet, most business owners don't hire salespeople. Gym owners hire coaches. Butchers hire assistant butchers. Chefs hire prep cooks. Instead of hiring to fill the holes in their business, founders try to duplicate themselves. And that's okay IF the founder plans to take on the sales role, but most never do. So if you don't have a dedicated salesperson on your team, let's think about it another way. Who's in charge of solving your clients' problems?

I want someone to tell me what to do most of the time. Better yet, I want them to just do it for me. I don't want to figure out how to change the oil on my new truck. I don't want to repair the roof on my cottage or replace the chain on my chainsaw. I want someone to say, "I've got this. What's your credit card number?" If you own a gym, your clients don't want to figure out nutrition on their own. (They've probably already failed at it.) They don't want to figure out how to avoid an injury. They don't want to figure out how to do a power clean correctly or how to climb a rope. They want you to solve the problem. That, my friend, is selling. And in the Founder phase, it's your job.

So what's your sales goal?

SET YOUR SALES GOAL

First, you need to measure your gross profit margin. The easiest way is to record the gross revenue from your business. For example, let's say you made $33,000 in sales last month. Then subtract out your fixed costs. We ask business owners to aim for fixed costs of 22 percent of their gross or less.

Now subtract your payroll from your sales. Everything that's left after subtracting your fixed costs and staff payroll is your gross profit margin. Your pay is included in your gross profit margin. We aim for a 33 percent gross profit margin, and in the service industry, that's pretty good. It's not amazing, but it's a start. (For more help with this breakdown, I recommend reading *Profit First* by Mike Michalowicz.)

After you've calculated your gross profit margin, you're

going to project the total revenue that you need to reach your goal. If your profit goal is to make $100,000 next year and your profit margin is 33 percent, then you need to gross $303,031 in your business.

If you need to gross $303,031 next year, and after doing some quick arithmetic, you're thinking, "Uh-oh, I can't possibly serve that many people!" That's okay. I believe in and teach a stratified model, which means diversifying your revenue streams.

That means looking at your clients, finding out exactly what they want, and then asking yourself, "How can I help them more?"

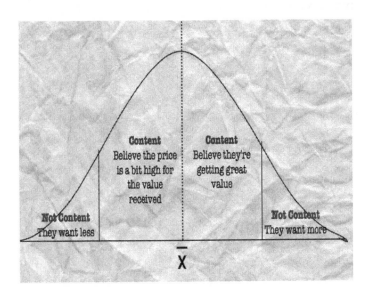

The clients of any business have a predictable purchasing pattern. Buyers tend to fall on a bell curve.

Ten to 20 percent of your clients want to pay less (or want less of your service) than what they're currently getting. They're probably not your ideal clients and will move on soon.

Around 30 percent of your clients are perfectly content. They think what they're getting is worth what they're paying.

Another 30 percent believe they're getting great value, that they're actually paying less than what they're getting in return. You love these people.

Finally, 10 to 20 percent of your clients want more from you. They want to pay for more, and they'll go looking elsewhere if they're not getting it from you.

The stratified model considers each of these buyers and builds layers of service for them. For example, when I opened my first gym, there were hundreds of people in my city who wanted to get fit. Some of those people wanted access to a gym and didn't care about the quality or efficacy of their workouts. These people weren't on my map because I had a coaching business.

Some of my clients wanted to spice up their workouts, so they chose to attend six-week challenges and boot-camps between their "normal" gym routines. These people fell on the left side of my bell curve: they were mostly transient and would sign up only if they perceived a short-term deal. Other clients wanted CrossFit groups. They were happy to attend a few times every week and be guided through an effective workout in a class setting. They were content to attend these groups for years.

Some clients wanted a bit more, and they would attend specialty coaching clinics, do a little personal training (our premium service), and buy every T-shirt we could design. And finally, my top clients chose our premium service (one-on-one training, nutrition design, and custom homework plans.)

When I decided that I needed to earn $325,000 from my gym to meet my goals, I considered my four primary revenue streams and built my forecast on that. For example, if my gross profit margin was 50 percent, then I needed to sell $650,000 worth of services every year, or $54,166 per month.

Twenty percent (or $10,833.20) would come from high-turnover programs, like six-week bootcamps.

Thirty percent (or $16,249.80) would come from people who only did CrossFit groups.

A further 30 percent would come from people who did mostly CrossFit groups but also specialized their training with our other options.

The last 20 percent (or $10,833.20) would come from clients who chose our premium one-on-one training option.

To make the numbers even more granular, I would break down the number of clients or programs I would need in each category. Our premium service offered a dozen one-on-one training sessions per month that cost $779. To reach my goal of $10,833.20, I would have to sell fourteen of those packages per month. So that was my goal.

HOW MANY CLIENTS DO YOU NEED?

Theoretically, you can maintain about 150 relationships. This is called "Dunbar's number," and it's a widely accepted anthropological estimate.

After 150 relationships, you start to forget important details about people. You struggle to keep clients because you can't remember important things about them. But if you can maintain 150 solid relationships and build a stable business on that group, your life will be a lot easier. In the Founder phase, 150 clients is the target. The systems we've built (above) will allow an entrepreneur to deliver her service with consistency and care to 150 customers.

Moving up to three hundred—or three thousand—clients requires a new set of systems, staff, and entrepreneurial skillset. We'll learn those new skills in the Farmer section.

Building your service model around Dunbar's number makes the math conservative and simple. One hundred fifty isn't a scary number, and it gives you a clear target to use in your planning.

As a gym owner, I determined that I needed $54,166 in revenue per month, which meant that each client's average monthly revenue had to be $361.10. That's a high price for a gym membership, even at a premium-level CrossFit gym. But consider that 20 percent of my membership pays much more than the rest.

Subtracting the outliers on the right side of the bell curve, my gym needed to sell $43,332.80 in nonpremium memberships. And if the difference was covered by only 14 personal training packages, that left 136 clients to split up the bulk of my revenues. The new average was $318.62 per month—still high but more realistic.

If I did the same calculation with the center-right group

(the 30 percent of my clients who wanted a bit more from me), I could have brought that average down further until I settled on my average rate—my ARM target.

Finally, don't forget that the bottom 20 percent of your clients will pull your ARM down, leaving a higher burden for the rest to shoulder. This was part of the reason I didn't offer discounts at my gym.

But what if you're selling a low-priced service, like $20 haircuts?

The simple math says you'll need far more volume. But even if your total client count doubled to 300 every month, it's still far easier to keep your existing clients than to find 300 new ones every month. That calls for systemization and consistency—maybe even automation: a client books next month's haircut as they're leaving, and your system automatically sends them appointment reminders. Build these into your client journey map.

To sum up: know what you want. Understand *why* you want it. Then calculate how you'll get it.

HOW TO CHARGE WHAT YOU'RE WORTH

Do you know what you're worth? More importantly, do you know how to get others to pay you what you're worth?

Here's how to make sure you're getting the money you deserve.

Be worth it. This sounds a bit backhanded, but the top reason many entrepreneurs can't charge more is that they're not worth more. Your value to a client doesn't come from what you know; it comes from how you make them feel.

Give every client one-on-one attention. You're serving a room full of individuals, not one entity with multiple parts. Or maybe you have thirty clients booked into your clinic today. Don't forget to have a personal interaction with each of them, and do not treat them as mere problems to solve. You don't have a sprained ankle and three sore backs in your schedule. You have Mary, Bill, Adam, and Steve.

Review their goals in person several times per year. How can you lead them if you don't know where they want to go?

Look like a professional. Dress better than your clients. Wear a "staff" shirt. Don't sip coffee while working with them. Run to fetch equipment. Smile, whether you feel like it or not.

Give them your undivided attention. Stay off your

phone. Don't carry on a conversation with others while coaching a one-on-one client. Don't coach "the room" but each person within the room.

Establish your expertise...but don't barf it all over them. Use one-to-two technical terms every session—no more, no less. Teach them more than any other coach in town, and they won't have a reason to leave. Give them a taste of future knowledge every session. Tell them the next step in whitening their teeth, and they'll look forward to it.

Don't give discounts or "sales." Your current clients are more important than any future ones. Is it worth risking them to bag a few extra sales? Price fluctuations erode trust, undermine consistency, and encourage price shopping. And they could cost you more than they bring in. Everyone deserves the same excellent service, and they should pay the same rate for it.

Base your rate off your service...not your competition. After doing thousands of one-on-one business evaluations with entrepreneurs in all industries, I can promise you this: your competitor probably had no idea how to price his service. Why place your business on the same shaky foundation by copying or, worse, pricing yourself cheaper than him?

Know who your clients are. Who is your best client? I

can't answer that question for you, but I can help you figure it out.

- You are probably not your best client.
- Your best clients come from the top 10 percent of professionals in your area.
- They make more than you do but have different constraints (schedule, family, stress).
- Your best clients have different goals than you do (fat loss, stress reduction, "turn off my brain").

In the Farmer section, we'll do an exercise called "Apples" to determine who your best clients are and exactly what they want from you.

Stop projecting your budget onto your clients. They make more than you do (for now). They will pay more than you would (for now).

Know what establishes value and what erodes it. Your list will be specific to your business, of course, but here are a few considerations to get you started:

- Price anchors establish value.
- Starting appointments on time establishes value.
- Professional caregivers establish value.
- Clear, attractive branding establishes value.
- A good website establishes value.

- Shiny equipment and floors establish value.
- Dirty bathrooms erode value, but they don't *create* value. They're just essential. No one looks for the lawyer with the cleanest bathrooms, but they'll quit the lawyer with the dirty ones. The same goes for not answering the phone or returning emails. These aren't bonuses; they're foundations.

Set a limit. The law of supply and demand applies to your business. You have limited supplies of attention, time, and space, so build your prices, staff needs, and purchases with that limit in mind. Recruit and reject clients and staff with that limit in mind too. Don't chase infinity.

Live up to it every second. A client's experience is only as good as their last exposure. What you know doesn't matter. How you make them feel does. Solving your clients' problems and making them feel great are cornerstones of sales in the Founder stage.

THE FOUNDER'S ROLES

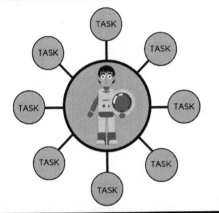

FOUNDER PHASE HIERARCHY

At this early phase, your team is small—it may be just you—but whether yours is a team of one or three, be ready to wear (almost) every hat. The founder is the hub of her company, its lead strategist, operations manager, driver of motivation and accountability, and its chief evangelist. In the Founder stage, the entrepreneur does it all herself. She bakes the cookies and coaches the CrossFit classes. If she DOES hire a staff person, she's usually micromanaging them to the point of near duplication instead of working on higher-value roles. There's one more hat she'll need to wear in addition to the rest: the model.

The founder must set the example. She must conform to the behavior she wants her staff to exhibit. She must obey her own rules. She must be a living example of the gold standard.

Before she can replace herself in any role, she must demonstrate perfect execution of that role to her staff. The quality of your service can be measured by how you do it when no one is watching. But staff is always watching. They'll rise only to the lowest acceptable standard set by the owner. Staff will do as the owner does.

As the founder moves toward the Farmer phase, she must begin to practice leadership. And the two words that define leadership are "Follow me."

A good leader models excellence, and they do it consistently.

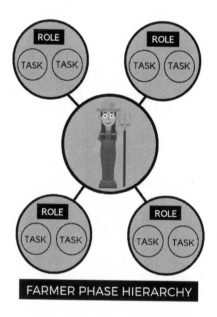

FARMER PHASE HIERARCHY

If you're a *South Park* fan like me, you're familiar with the underpants gnomes. The underpants gnomes are really good at stealing underpants, and they have a business plan: to steal underpants from kids and then to profit from it. Their business model is simple. Step one, they collect underpants. Step three, they profit. The whole "underpants gnomes" episode is dedicated to asking, "What's step two?"

It seems funny to think, but this is where a lot of entrepreneurs get stuck. It's certainly where I was when running my first gym. I was really, *really* good at coaching, getting people fit, and helping them lose weight. I could make them stronger. I could help clients with bad knees and those coming back from injury. I just wasn't good at getting to profit. Like the underpants gnomes, I needed to figure out my step two.

At first, I believed it was to get better and better at coaching, but that wasn't true. Pursuing excellence at fitness made me a great coach and gave me fitter, happier, healthier clients, but it didn't buy groceries. If I wanted my company to be profitable, I would also have to pursue excellence at business. And as I would learn, the foundational step to business excellence is consistency: how to do things without thinking about them and whether (and how) things get done automatically without your input. Consistency is step two, and that means writing your playbook.

Your staff playbook contains the "how" of everything, and it's one of the most important documents you can have in your business. Here's how to build it.

Refer back to your Roles and Tasks sheet, listing each of the hats you wear on a daily basis and their associated tasks. Reread the task list as though you were planning to take a month away without phone or email contact and fill in any steps or pieces that might be missing. Think *micro*—everything from updating software to changing empty toilet paper dispensers. (For help with this assignment, I strongly recommend *The E-Myth* by Michael Gerber.)

Clearly describe the gold standard for each task. What's a "ten out of ten" phone conversation in your business? What's the perfect email response to a question about your rates? Record those and include templates when you know what works.

Include text, pictures, screen-capture videos, and role-playing exercises. Make the clearest possible picture of what "excellence" means in your business. Then make sure you and your team deliver to that standard.

On top of your operational consistency, you must build a solid base of service. You have to believe that your business exists to help people, not to sell people. You need a "why" that sticks.

THE "STICKY WHY"

We need emotional reasons to hit any goal. The way we measure progress in Two-Brain mentoring clients is not how much they make. Instead, we ask:

- What will you learn this year?
- Where will you go this year?
- How much more time will you spend with your family this year?
- How will you upgrade your lifestyle this year?

One client responded:

> "I don't care what I make. But I want my wife to be able to walk into any store and buy anything she wants without looking at the price tag."

I found that goal inspirational. Here is one of mine. We shuttle kids to school and hockey and guitar practice non-stop. My wife drives all the time, and I wanted to buy her a new car. My goal was that she could walk into a car dealership, pick out whatever car she wanted, and pay for it on her debit card. A few months later, she did just that, and it felt amazing to me. She loves this vehicle. I like it too. It's great for napping in while she's just driving me around.

So what are your goals? And I'm not just talking about

a one-word answer or something vague like "financial security." I want you to come up with something you can visualize as easily as I can picture my wife walking into the car dealership. That's the key to making it stick.

Start with your **educational goal**. What are you going to learn next year? It might be something business-related or it might be knitting. It might be the guitar. It might be accounting. Or marketing. Whatever your goals, I want you to write them down.

The ability to take time away from work is a good way to measure a business's success, so I give entrepreneurs in our program a **travel goal** to take five days away without contacting their company at all. We need to make sure that the boat will float without them so that when they get back, they can work at a higher level. That's your next goal to consider: Where will you travel next year? Will you go to Disneyland? Will you go overseas? Maybe that ski trip you've been talking about for years?

The third is a **lifestyle goal**. What needs an upgrade this year? Is it your house? A new car? Do you want to get a pool for your kids? What kind of lifestyle do you want to create for them?

I volunteer to coach kids' hockey. Every now and then, I get to talk to Chuck, the father of one of my little players.

He is only in town about one weekend a month because he goes way up north to the bottom of the arctic circle and works in a pit mine. It's not a fun job. When he comes home, though, Chuck is all smiles. He tells me, "It's going to be a great Christmas this year." His lifestyle goal is for his kids. He's going to spoil them.

The last goal to write down is your **service goal**. Who will you help this year? What cause really resonates with you?

For me, that is helping kids and entrepreneurs. I always want to spend more time coaching kids, helping kids, and giving to kids. While you're thinking about your service or cost goals, I'm going to tell you about my "hockey misfits."

We live in a rural area, and hockey opportunities for kids are mixed. Sometimes there aren't enough kids to form a team. Sometimes there are too many kids to fit onto one squad. Last year, we had more kids than positions, and it looked like only the best players would make the team.

At the last minute, we managed to scrape up eleven kids—the minimum you need for a hockey team—for a second squad so that everyone who wanted to play got a spot. We had to talk a kid into playing goalie and put a little girl who had never skated before on defense, but we made it work. However, there was still their equipment to consider.

Every hockey team should have two jerseys: one for home games, and one for away games. The league couldn't buy our new team two jerseys each or enough ice time for practices. But I could. My wife and I became the unofficial team sponsors, and we were thrilled to buy these kids new jerseys, more ice time, warm-up suits—all the stuff the pros get.

My good friend Keith, a grizzled old hockey expert who just loves the kids, volunteered to coach the team. When I showed up to the first practice, he said, "Well, you're coaching too. Go get your skates." So three times every week, I skated with the kids, and we had a blast. It wasn't convenient to attend every practice. I was always tired the next day. I missed out on some great business opportunities because I couldn't miss their games. And it wasn't cheap. But my service goals were fulfilled.

After you write your service goals, we're ready to ask, "Do you have to modify your profit goal because of these REAL goals?"

It's important that you form an emotional connection to these goals instead of just saying, "I want to profit because I need to make more money." What will you learn? Where will you go? What will you upgrade? Who will you serve? Now you have a reason to profit. Now you have a sticky "why."

MOTIVATION FOLLOWS SUCCESS

Knowing the route to your goals isn't enough. After spending two decades in the fitness industry, I promise knowledge isn't the problem for most people. Motivation and accountability are the problems. After you've set your goals, you need to break them down into actionable chunks. Create habits (that's personal consistency) that will keep you focused and lead to success.

In the Tinker section of this book, I'll coach you through habit formation. For now, here's an advanced look at two tools that can keep you motivated to pursue your goals through the chaotic Founder phase. They're called "gap theory" and "bright spots." Gap theory is a system of breaking down goals into easily achievable steps, and bright spots is the practice of personal reflection on small wins.

George Loewenstein, a professor at Carnegie Mellon University, developed the gap theory in the 1990s. Its basic premise is that the closer you are to a goal, the more irresistible it becomes. Gap theory is the reason you don't walk out on a movie with five minutes left or throw away a book when you're in the last chapter.

If I needed to sell fourteen premium packages per month at my gym, I would write a big "14" on the whiteboard in my office. Every time I sold a package, I would enjoy erasing the number and writing "13" in its place. But if I got frustrated, I'd make the goal even smaller: I'd write a "4" on the whiteboard and make that my goal for the week. Or even a "1," and make that my goal for the day.

I gave my staff permission to do the same. And at the end of every week, we reviewed our bright spots: a short list of what went right that week. The practice of reflecting on small wins with gratitude is a huge motivator. That will be covered more extensively in Part Three, but the bright spots strategy is one of the few we use with every single client. It's that effective. No goal should ever be discarded, even when it seems unreachable; instead, it should be divided into smaller goals.

Planning takes time. Building replicable systems and recording best practices take time. But as an entrepreneur, this is your real work.

THE FOUNDER'S ROLE PROGRESSION

As a founder, you must establish the value of every role in your company and, over time, replace yourself in the lowest-value role. This is essential practice. You will have to define each role well, create a contract for the role, extrapolate an evaluation for the role, and go through the hiring process. Then use the time saved to work on a higher-value role. After three months, evaluate ROI (new revenue generated minus the cost of the replacement) and make changes as necessary. With each role you replace yourself in, you'll move closer to the Farmer stage.

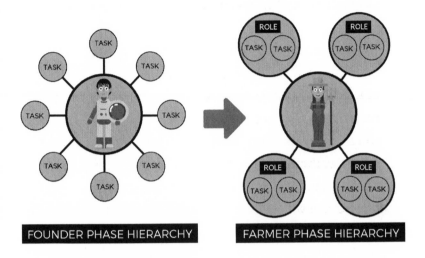

FOUNDER PHASE HIERARCHY

FARMER PHASE HIERARCHY

THE FOUNDER'S MENTOR

Lack of planning and lack of systems are the two biggest handicaps of most entrepreneurs. But other problems are often holding them back, and they're usually rooted in the founder's mindset.

Mindset can be trained, like your leg muscles or your focusing power. We publish mindset training tips on TwoBrain.com every day, and our program includes training for cognition and physical fitness. I'll share many of those techniques in the Tinker section of this book, but for now, here is the most common way an entrepreneur's own mind betrays her success.

She projects her budget, feelings, and opinions onto her clients. She sees herself as her own best client and believes she's serving 150 people with the same budget and worldview. Of course, an entrepreneur in the Founder stage is probably earning less than most of her clients. Her worldview—and her budget—isn't the same as theirs.

Some entrepreneurs look at the average family income in their city and build their rates and services from that arbitrary number. If I took the average demographic income in my city—a depressed steel town—I'd be pretty discouraged. But luckily for me, the mean average salary in my city is irrelevant.

Not every person in my city can pay what I need to charge. And that's fine. If I try to focus on everyone, I'll focus on no one. I focus on the top 10 percent of all earners in my city: the lawyers, the doctors, and the teachers. In my city, a lot of families are struggling. I try to help them by making donations to support services and volunteering to help their kids, but I'm not donating my business to them. I'm not donating my livelihood because then I can't help anyone. I didn't arrive at this understanding on my own, and it's not just my willpower that makes me adhere to it. I've got someone looking over my shoulder, looking for the changes I said I'd make, asking, "Did you do that yet?"

That person is my business mentor. After realizing the

power of mentorship to save my business, and then grow it, I founded TwoBrain.com to mentor other entrepreneurs. Over the next ten years, Two-Brain Business will mentor 1,000,000 entrepreneurs. This will be my legacy: tens of millions of jobs, multigenerational wealth, and a diversified world economy. Millionaires have mentors; startups have mentors. The great commonality among all good entrepreneurs is their willingness to ask, "Who has already solved this problem before me?"

So that's what you need to do at this stage: find yourself a mentor.

CORE CONCEPT: FITNESS

"Fitness" is commonly used to describe physical readiness and ability. However, entrepreneurs need more than physical fitness: we need to measure our fitness in skills like mental acuity, productivity, leadership, and resilience. "Fitness" in the entrepreneurial sense is the readiness and ability to perform work.

The five fitnesses of entrepreneurship are as follows:

- **Mental acuity**—An entrepreneur needs the potential to zoom out and see the big picture, also to focus on specific details without distraction. Entrepreneurship requires memory skills and cognitive dexterity.

- **Productivity**—Entrepreneurs need the energy to work long hours and finish on a timetable. While an employee typically fits their work into a schedule, a founder's work is done when it's done and not before. An entrepreneur has a task priority; a staff member has a time priority.
- **Leadership**—Despite the ups and downs, an entrepreneur must embody success to motivate his team. This means modeling success, communicating in ways that inspire action, and optimizing her team's efforts.
- **Resilience**—The mental fortitude to overcome barriers and build an "anti-fragile" business. Resilient entrepreneurs can withstand pressure to protect their service, income, and family.
- **Physical**—A business owner must appear fit, have an effective method for dealing with stress, create time for introspection, and be healthy enough to make good decisions. Physical fitness creates a buffer to aging and chronic disease. It improves focus and memory. Physical fitness improves confidence, which is critical to leadership and resilience.

For this reason, we place physical fitness at the foundation of the other "fitnesses." Physical fitness improves the readiness and ability to perform at all other necessary tasks. This is the 20 percent of your time that will form the foundation for the other 80 percent. For example, exercise improves mental acuity through faster memory recall by removing the fog of stress, sharpening your focus, and granting the ability to make connections between ideas.

Physical fitness also increases productivity by extending your endurance. "Large loads, long distances, faster" is the motto of many CrossFit gyms, and while most entrepreneurs no longer haul concrete, the ability to sit all day without injuring your back requires strong trunk musculature.

Less visible are the physical reactions to stressful situations. When a leader is given bad news, does she slump forward and put her head in her hands, or does she maintain good posture, tilt her chin up, square her shoulders, and take bad news in stride? The ability to face challenges can be forged in the gym. Likewise, when things are good, an athletic leader knows to stay grounded and humble because they're familiar with winning and losing. Resilience is the hardest "fitness" to qualify, but it's gained through exposure of "up" times and "down" times. That's a trainable skill. So is the ability to take a long view when problems arise. And the best way to train these skills at low risk is in the gym.

THE PRINCIPLES OF PEAK PHYSICAL PERFORMANCE

It's easy to get bogged down in the ins and outs of optimal

performance, especially if you turn to Google to find your answers. Fortunately, the foundational principles of peak performance are clear.

Set a schedule. Your body performs best in a three-days-on-one-day-off pattern. Start there. If, like me, you require slightly more rest, shorten the number of "days on" appropriately (three on, one off, two on, one off, repeat).

Vary your workouts. You need constant variety and bright spots to encourage activity. If your workout feels routine, you probably won't stick with it long.

Compound movements like the deadlift and squat train huge groups of muscles at once. Isolation exercises, which are primarily done on machines, take many times longer to complete and don't trigger the same metabolic or hormonal benefits. High-Intensity Interval Training (HIIT) is more effective at reducing stress and creating cardiac benefits than long, slow aerobics (cardio). But you also need exercise in a relaxed, aerobic state to maximize your cognitive health. Don't exclude easy jogs or bike rides.

Eat with your blood sugar in mind. Your nutrition should be aimed at controlling your blood sugar. That means balancing the intake of proteins, carbohydrates, and fats. If your blood sugar is low, you can't think clearly.

If your blood sugar is high, you'll be distracted. I follow a Zone diet to regulate my blood sugar. I'm still tired by the end of the day, but I'm productive ALL day. I don't get the midafternoon dip unless my blood sugar levels are going up and down.

Have a coach. Personal training is excellent and so is coached group fitness. Either way, you need someone to take an objective look at your fitness every few months, compare your results with previous metrics, and alter your training plan as necessary. You don't have time to guess. You need a fitness mentor.

CrossFit checks all of these boxes for me, and I'm not alone. Nelson Dellis, four-time USA memory champion, told me, "When I do CrossFit, I feel confident. I feel good. I feel healthy, which in turn makes me feel good about myself, and everything just feels more on point."

Dellis uses CrossFit to prepare his brain for the hard hours of memory training he puts in, and we'll touch on some of those strategies in the Tinker section. For now, let's keep the focus on optimal fitness. Here's my training week.

I attend a CrossFit class on Monday, Wednesday, and Friday. It's usually the same dozen people, and if someone doesn't show up, they get a call from the others.

The coach optimizes the weights and reps I do, and the skill focus forces me to concentrate on just the exercise, instead of being distracted.

On the weekend, I bike, ski, or run a longer distance. On busy days, I take twenty minutes after my peak creative window to bring my thoughts back into focus. The cumulative stress of these "extra" sessions is small. They're not intense.

Each quarter, my coach and I review some metrics: my body composition and my blood work. Body composition (body fat, lean muscle, weight) gives me a gross picture of my overall fitness, but blood testing tells the real story: I can't fake my LDL score or wish away low testosterone. I can't hide high cortisol levels. As we've established, objective measurements are essential, and that is as true for the health of your body as it is for the health of your business. Based on my results, my coach will recommend changes to my workouts (timing, frequency, duration, load) and eating.

As you can see, building a system for your physical health is not much different than the steps you take to build good systems in your business. You have no excuse for skipping it. Same goes for your cognitive health.

As with physical fitness, it would be easy to get buried in the myriad ways to improve your cognitive fitness. Here are the essentials.

Working out the body also works out the mind. Memory, recall, and the ability to make connections are all critical skills, and they can all be improved through moderate aerobic activity lasting around twenty minutes.

We can't avoid intensity. Exercise that is intense enough to demand our full concentration is necessary for stress reduction. An activity that's too easy will permit distraction; challenging exercise allows our brain to rest from the rapid task-switching that makes us feel tired.

Focus and attention are trainable. So is the memory. And we can build a buffer against loss in both cases.

Novelty is as critical in cognitive training as it is in physical exercise. Doing a crossword puzzle every day is good; doing it twice per week, with other activities on other days, is better.

Challenges are more effective than drills. In other words, you need some kind of scoreboard so you can measure progress.

Longer-duration repetitive tasks, in which the body performs consistent and automatic movements, will allow the mind to be more creative. This is why you have your best ideas while driving or showering. "Thinking body, dancing mind" is a common mantra in prayer rituals and slow exercise practices.

Long-term continuity is the most important of all. Just as with fitness, it's most important just to keep going. Here's how I stick to my cognitive routine.

First, I use the writer's practice of "morning pages" to clear the clutter out of my mind. I start my day by writing 750 words, even if they're random. It was a struggle at first, but as my "writing fitness" improved, I felt compelled to write every morning. Now I can't go a day without it. When I'm writing fit, new ideas wake me up in the morning, and I enter the flow state easily.

I set myself up for creativity in the morning by giving myself a head start the day before. I end my session with an incomplete sentence: if I'm writing a blog post, I'll sign off without an ending. The next morning, the ability to just "fill in the gaps" is the tiny push that starts my rock rolling downhill again. It's a practice I stole from Ernest Hemingway.

Next, I practice memory. Simple names and faces tests

or card memorization drills fill this gap for me, but you can train your memory without devoting specific time to it. Here is Dellis's top tip for improving the memory of entrepreneurs:

> I like to play this game with people who think they have a bad memory is go into a party and tell yourself you're going to remember ten people's names. That's it. Just by saying that to yourself, you suddenly make yourself focused on it. It becomes a little bit of a game. It becomes competitive, and you will remember ten names, probably even more. I really encourage people to say for a second to themselves, "I have a good memory. I'm going to just try it." By doing that, you'll pay attention, and you will see your memory improved.

When you see the results of memory training, you'll be encouraged to devote specific time to improve your memory even more. Dellis laid out clear instructions to get started:

> Let's do something a little different. Nelson is not the most common name, so if you met a Nelson, I would think of, and this is typically what people think of, is either Nelson Mandela, Nelson from the Simpsons—as a character—or a full nelson—this wrestling move—and these are all different things that we could visualize.

But Dellis explained, it's not enough to just come up with

a picture. You need an "anchor," something that stands out about the person. In his example, Dellis used his height:

> I'm tall, I'm six foot six, so if you met me, you'd notice I was tall. Nelson Mandela is the picture for my name, so you would somehow associate it.

The final step is a little story to link the picture with the anchor. And, as Dellis demonstrated, no story is too outlandish:

> Maybe you could picture Nelson Mandela sitting on top of my head because I'm tall and he wants to give a speech to many people, so he's sitting on my head to get a vantage point. I'm to look down on these people and then inspire them from above. That's the process. It's really just coming up with a picture and finding a way to store that information.

As a business owner, you must consider yourself a mental athlete. That means constant training and practice. As you mature as an entrepreneur, you'll need different strategies to grow as a leader, both in body and brain. A fitness bedrock is crucial to you in every stage. Without a tool to manage stress, buffer cortisol, trigger happy hormones, and create perspective, you're more likely to feel like a martyr.

"My staff never cleans up before they go home."

"Our front office is a pig sty!"

"No one returns phone calls or emails quickly."

"NO ONE cares except for ME!"

Moving to higher-value roles means moving from front-line delivery to a manager. To reach the next stage of entrepreneurship—farmer—you're going to need to manage more than yourself. If you struggle to get consistent action from your staff, there are two possible causes. The first probable cause is your process. The second probable cause is your people.

PROCESS PROBLEMS VS. PEOPLE PROBLEMS

If anyone on my staff is failing to perform at their highest level, I first assume it's my fault. The process isn't clear enough for them. So I ask myself, "Have I told them exactly what to do and how to do it?"

As founders, we frequently assume that everyone knows what we do or that our knowledge is "common sense." But, of course, that's not the case. No one knows how to write a compelling quote for a client until we tell him how.

Often, our instructions are too complex or contain gaps that our own brains skip right over. I once had a cleaner named Steve. His checklist said, "Mop the floors." He did, but he didn't use any soap because I didn't write, "Pour a cup of soap into the hot water." The dirty floors were my fault. Steve was just following my poor directions.

If I've told the staff person clearly how to do a job, and they're not meeting expectations, the next question I ask myself is: "Have I shown them what 'perfect' means?"

To me, "on time" means fifteen minutes early—at a minimum. But to a teenager, "on time" might mean two minutes late. If my front desk staff arrives at two minutes after nine on the weekend, and I've only told them to be "on time," I'm allowing a subjective consideration into my process. So if you're running into similar process problems, revisit your playbook and look for missing steps. Clearly spell out the gold standard in all work. If possible, take a picture. "Here's what a clean office looks like." No one can live up to an imaginary standard.

If someone on my team knows the gold standard and still fails to meet it, I ask myself the third question: "Have I reviewed their performance with them?"

If I haven't told the staffer that their work is subpar, they probably think it's just fine. Over 80 percent of drivers claim to be better than average because our egos won't let us believe we're bad at anything. Your staff is the same way. If you don't rate their performance, they will assume it's good enough. Schedule quarterly reviews for all staff. Do it in advance. And give them the scorecard (your evaluation form) on the day of their hire.

Finally, if I'm sticking to an evaluation schedule and they're still failing, I ask myself a fourth question: "Do they have an emotional reason to succeed?"

I can tell Steve to take out the garbage because it's his job. I can impose my authority and threaten punishment. But we're all human and driven by irrational desires. At 9 p.m., when Steve is tired and wants to make it home in time to watch *Shark Tank*, he might skip the garbage takeout. It might not even be a conscious decision.

My job is to make him see the consequence of that choice through the eyes of others. If Steve doesn't empty the garbage tonight, Mary will have to do it in the morning. She'll be finishing his job for him. Just as your mom used to guilt you into doing work by doing it for you while you watched, you need to give your staff an emotional reason to succeed. Ask them, "How will it affect the other staff if your work isn't done?" or, "What impression will our clients have if the floor isn't clean?" or, "What will the buyer think if you misspell his name on the invoice?"

If the four questions above don't solve the issue, you don't have a process problem; you have a people problem. The wrong person is doing the wrong job.

Let's say Steve is still failing to meet the standards I've set for his role. I know he's a great person, so the issue may be that he is doing a job that doesn't optimally challenge him.

First, ask, "Does he have a clear view of his future in the company?" In other words, can Steve see how his progress in this role will affect his opportunities later? Does he believe he's stuck cleaning the kitchen for life, or does he know it's a short-term step before being promoted to assistant manager? Make it a habit to set up regular goal-review meetings for your staff.

The second question is: "Does their future position depend on success in this position?" Meaning, am I judging Steve's worthiness to be a great coach on his ability to sweep the floors? No one is perfect at everything—not me, not you, and not your staff. The person could just be in the wrong role. I am NOT a great cleaner, but I'm a good motivator. Placing me in a cleaning role won't make me happy unless I see the big picture and my place in it with a time line for advancement.

The last question is: "Will this person be part of the team that takes us to the next level?" The people who got you *here* might not be the same people who get you *there*. It's true of your staff, and true of you. While you're busy developing your entrepreneurial skills with your mentor, your team might not be doing the same. And that's okay. They might want to vacuum forever. Some people do. But when you move to the enormous warehouse without carpets, you'll need a new skillset. And if a staffer isn't ready to acquire the necessary skills, you have a new people problem. You should chart their career path—or their exit.

One of the greatest questions I've ever learned to ask is: "Do you still want to do this?" Surprisingly, the answer is sometimes no, and that's much better than "maybe" because it allows both the founder and her staff to move forward, even if it's not together. When your staff isn't living up to your expectations, first assume you have a process problem. But if you've satisfied all four of the questions above, you have a people problem. That's tougher but still solvable.

Of course, a founder's challenges don't always boil down to process or people. As a founder, sometimes the issue is *you*, your habits, or the myths you've accepted as truths.

THE HUSTLE IS A LIE

Have you read *Once a Runner* by John L. Parker? I'll tell you the gist of the story. Boy runs a lot. Does okay. Finds a mentor. Mentor says, "Run a lot more." The boy runs his legs off. Breaks the four-minute-mile mark.

It's a beautifully written book by an author who never ran a four-minute mile.

Unfortunately, many runners read the book as a training manual. They believe the way to run faster is just to run more. It's not true. The secret to running a four-minute-mile, as Roger Bannister (the first man to actually run a four-minute mile), is interval training. Bannister ran sets of 400-meter sprints to train, keeping his intensity up and spending his energy wisely.

I work with hundreds of entrepreneurs. Each one is a hard worker. They expect to get up early and work until dark. They embrace the work. Most believe (as I once did) that merely outworking everyone else will bring success.

It's not true.

The hustle isn't the goal.

The goal is the goal.

More time off is the goal. Paying off your house is the goal. Playing with your kids is the goal.

What's wrong with a strong work ethic? Nothing...unless it stops you from achieving what's really important. In other words, sacrificing intensity for volume. Let me give you an example that I hear all too often:

> "I'm at the office from 5 a.m. until 8 p.m., but I don't have time to do what you're telling me to do! And I don't have the money to pay anyone to help me."

After we calculate the value of the founder's time, it's clear they're working too much for too little. In some cases, they're opening up for a couple of early clients and making less than they'd earn at McDonald's. Sometimes they're paying a staff person $20 an hour and earning less than $15 in the same hour.

In that all-too-familiar example, the business owner is really business-owned. They'd do better to work at Walmart and volunteer their service for free on the weekends!

"Embracing the hustle" can be a bad strategy because it can prevent you from doing the things you should be doing. It's easy to fool ourselves into believing "more work" is the same as "better work," that volume equals intensity. It's not true.

Do your bathrooms need to be clean? Yes. Cleaned by

you? No. You're probably holding your business, your staff, and your clients back if you're performing every little role in the company. Work expands to fill the time allocated to it. Stop wasting that time.

STAYING FOCUSED

There's treasure everywhere! Most entrepreneurs who book free consultations with Two-Brain Business have plenty of ideas. Their problem is a lack of time. They're trying to do five things at once, which means nothing is getting done. Here's how to stay focused on ONE goal at a time.

Get a mentor. All of my success has come while under the tutelage and focused guidance of a mentor. Seriously. It's important. My own mentor supplied most of the advice in this section.

Set annual goals. Break those goals into monthly targets. Break the monthly targets down by revenue stream. Now you have point B. Everything that doesn't move you closer to point B in a measurable way should be discarded from your daily business.

Calculate the value of your time. If you want to make $1,000,000 next year, you need to spend 2,000 hours doing $500-per-hour work. You do NOT have extra hours, so you CANNOT be doing $15-per-hour work if you plan to hit your goal. If you want to make $100,000 next year, every hour of work must be worth at least $50. No one is paying you $50 to scroll through your Facebook feed. Are you doing forty hours of $50-per-hour work *net* every week? What about that "class" of two people you're running at ten in the morning?

Know that "adding another thing from your cognitive overhead takes you away from your real goal." That's straight from my mentor, Dan Martell. You do not have unlimited bandwidth or focus. Every second you spend working on a task that doesn't directly impact your goal adds steps to achieving it.

Most side hustles are really a mental plan B. People start printing T-shirts because they don't trust their ability to succeed at running a gym. If your net on shirts is $5 per shirt, and you have to invest $1,000 in a heat press and twenty hours in design, wouldn't it better to spend that time on goal reviews with members? As Dan says, "People do this stuff because they don't trust that their primary thing is going to be awesome. They lack trust in their own ability to execute on plan A."

Keep a "next year" list. Write that new idea down on a special "get to it next year" whiteboard. That way, you're not trying to remember every opportunity, and you're not turning exciting stuff down. You're just saying, "Later." It helps clear the junk out and focus on your current goals.

Measure the potential ROI of your primary activity and compare everything else against it. A dollar invested in Catalyst in 2005 would be worth about $22 now. Why would I put that dollar in a mutual fund with a 7 percent return when I could make a 220 percent return by investing in myself? Time works the same way. Why invest in "side projects" when your core business can deliver SO much more?

In the Founder phase, it's imperative to maintain focus on ONE idea at a time. Later, when this business runs itself, when you're achieving a 33 percent profit margin (at minimum), and you meet the other Tinker phase prerequisites, you can come back and work on the next big idea.

THE PARALYZING EFFECT OF THE VOCAL MINORITY

Even when things are amazing, it's very easy for founders to focus on the "problem areas." Our brains are wired to detect flaws. We fixate on negative feedback even when it doesn't represent the average client. And when someone says they don't like a class time on our client surveys... well, we want to smash the whole puzzle and start from scratch, don't we?

Brian Alexander is one of the mentors at Two-Brain Business. He employs thirty coaches between two gyms and relies on his strong leadership style to inspire them to take the right action when they're out of his sight. Brian's crew was starting to report that "some of the members" had problems with "some of the services" or "some of the class times." These are always hard to pin down (*which* members? What *exactly* did they say?), but Brian has been through this before.

Over a year ago, Brian raised the rates at his gym and a small—but very vocal—minority of clients quit to make their point about the prices. Most have since come back, but at the time, Brian had to fight the temptation to back down from his core values and cave in to keep them. This is how he got through it and the lesson he shared with his staff:

> There will always be a small minority of people who complain about everything. For example, not including Spark [his bootcamp service] in unlimited memberships, or charging extra for specialty programs, or charging for nutrition advice, not having enough classes, CrossFit being too expensive. While we listen to everyone, we act according to our vision for the gym and don't let the 'loud minority' sway us, because we understand that they don't see the big picture we do.

When I hear, "Everyone is complaining," or, "Everyone thinks this," I know that "everyone" is not everyone. It is just the "loud minority." That loud minority, while welcome at our gym, isn't our perfect client. If we wavered on our position for every little complaint, we would have no direction. We'd have 100 different programs at 100 different prices and 100 concessions for each one.

We don't do that. We deliver fantastic service and experience. Those who appreciate that will stay, and the "loud minority" will leave eventually. It's a simple filter. What Brian and I have learned is that following the minority is a disservice to the majority. Just as it's essential to train your strengths, it's important to focus on your happy clients most of the time. Let me give you another example.

Videos that autoplay on Facebook and Instagram look really cool. Most people love them, and businesses that use video will have a tiny bit more sway over those that don't. Facebook has data showing higher conversions on pages utilizing a video cover. You can turn the video into an ad, then build a custom audience for viewers, and then a retargeting campaign. The possibilities abound.

But two or three people on my Facebook feed say, "I hate it when videos autoplay on my phone." They can turn autoplay off but probably don't know it (and frankly, some of these people invite me to play Candy Crush on a daily basis). But still, it's tempting to turn off an impactful tool because a tiny minority says so.

Perfect is the enemy of good. Not everyone will like everything you do. That's fine. Your best clients will thank you for your consistency...and for giving them what THEY love.

MARTYRDOM: THE OPPOSITE OF A PERFECT DAY

"10:19 p.m. Leaving the gym. Missed my girls, but my 5 a.m. class will have clean floors. All about the hustle!"

"Working from the city today...it reminds me of those ten looong years I spent coming in here for my day job. Those days...when I was earning 5x what I am today but was 5x UNHAPPY. These days...earning 5x less but am 100x HAPPIER. It's not about how much you HAVE. It's about how much you ENJOY the seconds..."

"A bunch of members quit when this new box opened down the road. They've got daddy's money and all the toys. But I'm just going to keep coaching my clients even better even if it means my wife has to go back to work."

Scroll through the Instagram and Facebook pages of business owners for an hour today, and I guarantee you'll find one of these. I know because that's where I found all three.

All came from excellent owners who are changing their clients' lives.

All came from founders who had thousands of followers on social media.

All came from entrepreneurs who deserve better. All came from dads whose kids deserve to see them at bedtime. All came from husbands whose wives deserve to live without stressing over the grocery bill.

This has to stop.

Here are the myths that lead to martyrdom and what to do about them.

No one can do it like I can. You might be the best coach in your gym, but I doubt you're the best cleaner. Or the best Instagrammer, best programmer, best website builder, best writer, or best bookkeeper. You're definitely not the best at ALL of them.

There's no money to pay me. Yes, there is. If you pay yourself first, you'll get paid. Your business is not successful until it can support you. That's its purpose. Don't get in the habit of working for free.

Leaders eat last. A humble statement repeated by those

who can feed their flocks and still have a feast left over. The statement should really be, "Leaders eat." Let's say you're flying to Australia. It's a twenty-hour flight, and the catering crew forgot to load the plane. One of the stewards finds a single sandwich in the fridge. Who gets it? I'd give it to the pilot because if he goes hungry, the rest of us go into the ocean. There is no glory, no sainthood, in depriving yourself while your staff gets paid.

I need to pay off all my debt before I take a paycheck. Also false. Cash flow is more important than your annual balance sheet, especially in a startup. When I had to buy my partners' share of the debt in 2010, I called the bank and asked to consolidate my loans and spread them out over a longer time frame. I was ashamed and embarrassed and felt like a failure. My loan officer said, "Oh, you've never taken a cash flow loan? Everybody does that."

My monthly payments went down, my stress level went way down, I stopped missing paychecks, and I found some breathing room. Then I started building my business and paid off the loan in three years instead of ten... but only when I had the money. Sacrificing your earnings to pay off a low-interest loan faster doesn't hurt the bank. It just hurts you.

Everyone will forgive my exhaustion, hot temper, and poverty because they'll respect my hard work. This is the biggest lie I've ever told myself, that I'll be respected, damn it, because I'm such a hard worker.

But my kids still missed me at bedtime.

My wife would rather have had me home and not exhausted.

My clients would rather have hung around a successful person.

We're all depending on you: your kids, your wife, your clients, and even other entrepreneurs. We don't care if you become a millionaire. We care that you stay healthy. And we want you to eat the damn sandwich.

"PERFECT" IS THE ENEMY OF "GREAT"

Before we move into the Farmer section of this book, I want to talk to you about perfection.

I know you're waiting for the ideal time to quit your job and open your business. Or start a blog or hire a helper. Well, here's the great news: there's no perfect time. There never will be. Here's the bad news: there's no perfect time, and there never will be.

Maybe you're waiting for more revenue to hire more

staff before you start working on goals and roles. Perhaps you're waiting for ten more clients before you hire a mentor. You can choose to wait: for a sign, for an order, something that makes the choice for you. Or you can just start.

In the final section of this book—the Thief phase—I'm going to tell you, step by step, how to do what I've done: start with nothing and end up wealthy and retired before age forty-five. I call the process the Authority Ladder. It's the path to becoming the best in your business, and then turning around to lead others. The process is simple, but not easy. And the first step is one of the hardest: giving up what you are to be all you can.

I've fallen off the ladder many times. But MOST people don't ever take the first step in their climb because they refuse to take their foot off the ground. They tell themselves they're waiting for perfect—the perfect time, the perfect partner, the perfect location—but really, they're just waiting for someone to make the decision for them.

My kids love to watch "talent searches" on TV at night. I'm sure you've seen these: talented children line up with their parents for DAYS, then do one high-pressure audition in front of a panel. If they do well, the panel gives them the green light to move to the next stage. Eventually, there's a finale, and the contestant with the most perfect performance is voted into stardom. But what the show doesn't measure is grit. The audience doesn't care about longevity. None of these winners will ever make it into a hall of fame, and though one might have a best-selling album, they'll never be the best. They'll never be an authority in music.

Dave Grohl *is* an authority in music. Grohl leads the Foo Fighters now, but he was the drummer for Nirvana before Kurt Cobain died and the band split up. In March 2013, Grohl was interviewed for *Sky Magazine*. He was asked what he thought about televised music contests. This was his response:

> When I think about kids watching a TV show like *American Idol* or *The Voice*, then they think, "Oh, okay, that's how you become a musician, you stand in line for eight f***ing hours with 800 people at a convention center, and then you sing your heart out for someone, and then they tell you it's not f***ing good enough." Can you imagine?

He went on...(I love this part):

> It's destroying the next generation of musicians! Musicians should go to a yard sale and buy an old f***ing drum set and get in their garage and just suck. And get their friends to come in, and they'll suck too. And then they'll f***ing start playing, and they'll have the best time they've ever had in

their lives, and then all of a sudden, they'll become Nirvana. Because that's exactly what happened with Nirvana. Just a bunch of guys that had some s***ty old instruments and they got together and started playing some noisy-ass music, and they became the biggest band in the world. That can happen again! You don't need a f***ing computer or the internet or *The Voice* or *American Idol.*

Grohl is talking about playing imperfect music on imperfect instruments with an imperfect group. He was never really best friends with Cobain or the other band members, but that didn't matter. He didn't have to love the songs or his bandmates. He just had to love playing.

My first book (*Two-Brain Business*) was a collection of blog posts I'd written over four years as a struggling gym owner slowly finding my way. One day, I was invited to speak at a seminar in Florida, and one of the other speakers was bringing a book to share. "Shoot," I thought, "guess I better have one too." So I pulled my favorite blog posts together and self-published the book online because it was cheaper than having it printed and bound at a copy store. I didn't have a table of contents, the cover was hand-drawn, there's a section 2 but no section 1, and it's the bestselling fitness business book of all time. It's sold over 20,000 copies worldwide. I sign autographs inside the front cover when I travel to seminars. The book still doesn't have a table of contents.

Perfect is the enemy of great.

Let's work away from perfect and get on with being great.

CASE STUDY: THE HARRIED HOSTESS

"I think I hate people." Louella's family has been in the restaurant business for three generations. She was raised in her grandmother's kitchen. She was serving tables before she started high school, and she's been greeting guests for over thirty years. When she called, Louella told me, "I just don't understand this younger generation. Nobody wants to work hard! And the minimum wage keeps going up. It's like these kids want something for nothing."

I asked her why she felt that way.

"You'll see," she said. "Come for lunch."

I love lunch, so I replied, "See you this afternoon."

I'm chronically early for things, so I arrived ten minutes before noon. Louella was clearly flustered: "Oh, I didn't expect you yet!" she looked around the room. There were empty tables, but her mind was already juxtaposing the lunch crowd on the filling restaurant. "Um, why don't we sit outside?" she said.

We did. I told her not to rush.

She said, "No, no, I should be fine. I have lots of staff working right now," and rolled her eyes. She hustled back inside to check her team.

I didn't see her again for fifteen minutes.

When she returned, she noticed that the wait staff hadn't delivered menus to our table, and that I didn't have anything to drink. "Are you kidding me?" she said, clearly exasperated, and burst back inside the restaurant to berate one of the waitresses. I couldn't hear what she was saying, but I could imagine. The flustered waitress came out right away, practically tripping over herself to take a drink order.

I could see Louella through the restaurant windows. She took a phone call, probably a reservation request. She frowned as she listened, pursed her mouth into a tight line and shook her head. I read her lips as she said "Nothing" to the caller, and when she caught me watching, she rolled her eyes. Then she held up a finger to show me she'd only be a minute. I signaled that I was fine. I was happy to sit out on the deck and sip lemonade.

Before she could leave the phone, however, some new patrons approached Louella to ask her for a table. She did the same scan as before and pointed outside. She looked as if she was daring them to say, "We prefer to eat inside," and when they hesitated, she grabbed menus and walked out onto the patio without looking back. The guests looked at each other, shrugged, and followed her. But the empty tables on the patio weren't yet set for lunch, so she smacked the menus down, apologized to the guests, apologized to me for taking so long, and went back inside to berate another waitress. She looked frazzled. She looked *mad*. And it was only twelve o'clock.

When Louella finally sat down at the table, I had eaten a sandwich and ordered espresso. "I'm really sorry to keep you waiting. What must you think of me?" She was really embarrassed. "But you see what I mean? The place would fall apart if I didn't do every little thing myself!" And then the dam burst. She talked for ten straight minutes about millennials and work ethic and kids who don't want to work. She talked about lazy help and impatient clients. Finally, she summed up by saying, "People!" and then taking a long drink of wine.

I waited for a moment and then said, "Louella, it sounds like you have a horrible job." I smiled, because I was half-joking. But only half.

"Yeah, well, my boss is a slave driver!" she said. She was obviously talking about herself.

"So why don't you quit?" I asked.

Louella didn't hesitate: "No way."

"How about you step away from hostessing?" I countered.

She paused, then nodded her head. "That might be a good idea."

Here are Louella's real problems:

1. She needs to get out of the way and let her staff—young, energetic, and happy—do their jobs. Even if they do their jobs less effectively than she does, they'll do them happier without her. And in the service industry, a smiling server is more important than almost anything else.
2. She needs to stop micromanaging. That's obvious. That means teaching her staff what to do instead of waiting for them to make the wrong decisions.
3. She must replace herself as hostess.
4. She should probably take a few weeks off.

In the restaurant business, the hostess is really the sales manager. They set up the patron and influence their purchase. The sales role is the hardest for most entrepreneurs to give up, but they must, or they'll never progress beyond Farmer phase. And many owners simply aren't the best salespeople for their own service.

Louella had begun to hate her job, and it showed. Her food is still good—heck, it's amazing—but Louella's attitude sours the sweetest dessert. As Maya Angelou wrote, "People will forget what you said, people will forget what you did, but people will never forget how you made them feel." Success in the restaurant industry, like the gym industry, the legal industry, and the preschool industry, isn't determined by how the food is plated, or even how it's priced. Success pivots on how people feel after a night out at your place. Louella might once have been the best hostess in town, but now it's time to fire herself from that role and be an entrepreneur instead.

I said, "Louella, tomorrow I'll take YOU out for lunch. We'll go somewhere else and talk about how to move you from founder to farmer. Don't be late."

CORE CONCEPT: THE REAL PATH TO SUCCESS

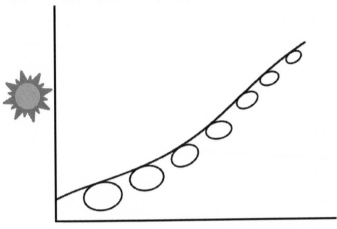

The REAL Path to Success

This is what the path to success looks like (extending to infinity).

You're going to make progress. Then you're going to backtrack *almost* to zero again. Then you'll make a bit more progress, and then you'll backtrack *almost* to the point you were last time. Progress, backtrack, progress, backtrack.

But here's the reason to keep going: every time you loop back, you won't go quite as far back as before. The loops get smaller. And you'll also start to notice that you're not backtracking quite as often as before. Someday you'll look up and think, "Wow, I've gone a whole year without any major problems." And when you have problems, thinking this way will help you keep your perspective.

Nikole, a mentoring client, coined the hashtag #high-classproblems. And I love the phrase because it reminds me that, while problems will never go away, they get smaller in magnitude and less frequent over time as long as you keep progressing. Many business owners don't. They get stuck in that first loop forever.

You won't. It's time to become a farmer.

ARE YOU READY TO BE A FARMER?

Have you determined your three key services or products?

Have you set your pricing, with at least three tiers?

Have you packaged some of your services together?

Have you determined pay rates for each role in your business?

Have you written out your processes, defined your gold standard, and built a playbook?

Do you have contracts for your staff and partners?

Have you hired a replacement for yourself in at least two roles?

Are you evaluating your staff?

Have you mapped your client journey?

Have you spelled out your intake process so anyone on staff can deliver it?

Have you practiced the sales process with your staff?

Have you started Affinity Marketing?

Have you calculated your basic metrics (ARM, LEG, and profit)?

PART TWO

—

FARMER

"There is a compelling tendency among novices developing any skill or art, whether learning to play the violin, write poetry, or compete in gymnastics, to quickly move past the fundamentals and on to more elaborate, more sophisticated movements, skills, or techniques. This compulsion is the novice's curse—the rush to originality and risk."

—GREG GLASSMAN, FOUNDER OF CROSSFIT

I spent last New Year's Eve with a friend named Mark. Mark's a farmer.

We sat at his handmade kitchen table drinking Mad Jack, both of us stifling yawns. I'd been up since 4 a.m., and Mark had been up all night, fixing power lines in -30° weather for his "real job." Mark works for the power company, but he's still a farmer.

Our wives were leaning against the kitchen counter, talking about a mutual friend who'd won the lottery in 2017. Half a million isn't enough to retire on, but it pays a lot of bills, and I asked Mark what he'd do with it.

"I'd farm until it was gone," he answered.

Most farms lose money. If you calculated the value of a farmer's time, each hour worked would be worth pennies or less. And yet Mark wears a shirt with a tractor on it. His kids' toys are all tractors. Look out any window in his two-story house, and you'll see a farm. Mark doesn't farm to make money. Mark makes money so he can be a farmer.

I know a lot of entrepreneurs like Mark: if they won the lottery today, they'd still show up to work at 6 a.m. tomorrow. In fact, it's one of the questions on our *Founder | Farmer | Tinker | Thief* test, and almost everyone gives the same answer: "I'd keep building my business."

(You can take the test at TwoBrain.com/test.)

Owning a business is more than just buying a job, and many of us take "day jobs" to support our entrepreneurial habit. We NEED our businesses to thrive. Our clients depend on our ability to make the business work. Our staff deserves success. Our kids deserve the life we want to give them. We don't do it just to make money. We do it because we're entrepreneurs.

If you own a business, you understand the plight of the farmer. Small businesses, like small farms, are continually battling high-volume corporate brands. We're outgunned and out-financed, but the quality of our product or service keeps us in the game. Many of us would spend our lottery winnings to prop up a failing idea if it came to it. Passion is not the problem. Profit is. We have to be profitable *now*.

Mark might never get the chance to go all in on farming, but as an entrepreneur, you have a responsibility to push your chips into the center of the table. You don't have the luxury of staying a founder forever.

It's time to focus, to systemize, to move to higher-value roles, and to make sure you're doing the *right* work instead of the work right in front of you. It's time to put profit first and extend your brand from "me" to "we." And it's time to plow forward in spite of your fear because if you're counting on your passion for coaching or making donuts to make your business a success, well...you might as well buy lottery tickets.

THE FARMER'S KEYWORD: CULTIVATION

At this point, you have planted the seeds and should

now focus on feeding and watering your crop and helping it grow. The Farmer phase has many goals, including improving your gross profit margin to 33 percent, creating a cash flow asset that can run itself, and limiting yourself to no more than forty hours per week within the business. It is also at this stage that you, as the business owner, should start to replace yourself in the lower-value roles.

THE FARMER'S #HASHTAG

If we were to sum up the Farmer phase in a hashtag, it might be #resilience, or maybe #growth. The farmer is attempting to elevate her platform and add support at the same time. This means building a retention strategy *and* a sales strategy, diversifying her revenue streams *and* improving her current service. Growing her crops, avoiding blight, focusing on her best clients, and attracting new ones. It's a lot to balance.

THE FARMER'S VALUES

In the Founder phase, the company's values were the values of the founder. Since he filled almost every role, the founder was able to deliver on his values while he baked the bread, while he served the customer, and while he swept the floors.

In the Farmer phase, the entrepreneur builds his team

around him. This means that his values must become the team's values. It means that delivery of those values must go from "me" to "we." And it means that some values might change. For example, "I personally inspect every pair of shoes that goes out our door" might change to "Every shoe that goes out our door meets my personal standards." The difference is more than phrasing: it's adoption.

If a farmer's team doesn't adopt his values, his vision won't be fulfilled. While consistency in delivery is most important, the intent with which your service is delivered is critical to your company's success. This is the difference between obeying the letter of the law and obeying its spirit. But values can't be dictated. They must be adopted. Your team members must feel like they have a hand in shaping and creating those values. They must take ownership.

DEFINE, THEN REFINE

There are two types of values:

- Aspirational: an inspiring vision of where we want this company to go.
- Authentic: how we want to work with each other and with our clients on a day-to-day basis.

Take the "values" exercise from the Founder phase, divide your staff into partners or small groups, and have each person walk through the exercise. What experiences and influences have shaped their value system? Have them share stories. Then ask, "What are the behaviors that support these values?"

Take their answer from "me" to "we": How can the company support those values with staff and clients? Define the limits of those values. What are some critical indications that the team has stepped away from them?

After you've established the values you'd like to adopt company-wide, follow up with these questions:

- What do we want to be when we grow up? What does the company look like in two years?
- What do we want to be to our customers? Who are our best clients?
- What do we want to be to our employees? Who are our current models?
- What do we want to be with our vendors and partners?
- What do we want to be to our investors?
- What do we want to be to our community?

Take the answers to those questions and the questions above, and write ten core values for your company. Express them in the third person and make sure everyone in the group agrees on the phrasing. Group common themes together—the shorter the list, the better—but don't condense them too much. Clarity is critical. Make each value statement as concise and as clear as possible.

Finally, determine how to deliver these values to future team members. Ask your staff:

- If someone new came into the company, how would you explain this statement to them?
- Will this be important three years from now?
- If you saw someone acting in a way that did not align with this value, what would you say to hold him accountable?
- If you looked around your team, what characteristics inspire you to want to be like them?

These shared values will go a long way toward establishing and maintaining a strong culture in your company even if you're not there to steer it.

THESEUS'S BOAT: MAINTAINING YOUR CULTURE WHILE REPLACING YOURSELF

After conquering Crete, Theseus and the young warriors of Athens journeyed home on a boat with thirty oars. Upon arrival, the boat was lifted up as a display of their triumph for hundreds of years.

A wooden boat will naturally rot over time, and over the years, each board of Theseus's ship was taken out and replaced as necessary until eventually none of the original boards remained. But the boat was still on display.

Plutarch asked, "Is it still Theseus's boat?" It's a question that applies to your business as much as it does to maritime artifacts. How does your business survive change, and how much change can it withstand before you no longer recognize it?

As you move to higher-value roles, you'll have to replace yourself in each area of your business. First, you'll stop mopping. Then you might cut back on coaching or posting pictures from your workouts. Your clients will eventually take notice.

I remember one of my favorite members, Kath, asking me, "Why do you run and hide in your office all day instead of standing on the floor and chatting with people like you used to?"

The answer, of course, was that my business wasn't growing while I was standing around for twelve hours talking to people. But I couldn't share that with Kath or any of my clients because they wouldn't understand it. From their perspective, everything was great. From mine, I was dead-broke, exhausted, and barely containing my constant frustration (and secretly ready to fold the business). People notice when you replace the planks. Does that mean you should let the boat rot to preserve its authenticity? Of course not.

Here's another (more recent) example of the Theseus's boat question.

A young boy inherits his grandfather's ax. He's inspired to become a lumberjack like his grandfather, so he starts chopping down a tree. Halfway through the tree, the handle of the ax breaks. So the boy replaces the handle and continues to chop. The ax head soon becomes dull. So the boy sharpens the head and notices there's not much edge left. So he buys a new head and finishes cutting down the tree. His father congratulates him for cutting down the tree with his grandfather's ax. But did he?

To the boy (and his father), he *did* cut down the tree with his grandfather's ax, even though both parts of the ax (the handle and the head) were new. In a literal sense, it wasn't his grandfather's ax at all. Grandpa had never touched that handle or sharpened that blade. But in a subjective sense, it was his grandfather's ax the boy used because the STORY made it so.

Your business isn't your logo. Your business is the feeling people get in your gym and the story they tell about it.

When clients are welcomed to class, are they greeted warmly by every coach, as you would do? If a client's bill isn't paid on time, are they treated kindly, as YOU would treat them?

The story binds the boat together. The boat is simply the symbol for the story. Your policies, your pictures, and your posts are all part of your story, and it's up to you to make sure it's being told the right way. And that means educating the other storytellers. If your staff doesn't know how to tell your story, they'll tell THEIR story. So give them a system—here's how you greet people, here's how you start the class, here's how you lead the warm-up—or the story will change.

John C. Maxwell wrote that you "can't reach the next level until you've completely replaced yourself at this level." He was talking about replacing planks in boats. For your legend to endure beyond its necessary parts, like Theseus's ship and the grandfather's ax, make sure your story is consistent. Doing so will enable you to tackle the farmer's work (and earn a farmer's rate).

THE FARMER'S KINGMAKER EQUATION

We don't rise to our opportunities; we fall to our level of preparation. Many entrepreneurs start the week with bold strides: they launch a new Facebook ad campaign or send a new product logo to their graphic designer. They do things that move the needle. By 2 p.m., they've completed their checklist and launched a brand-new service... and then their toilet gets clogged.

The entrepreneur looks around and asks, "Who's going to fix this toilet?"

A tumbleweed rolls through.

He quickly realizes, "It's me. I'm the only person willing and able to use a plunger." So the entrepreneur spends the next three hours plunging a toilet and cleaning up the water on the floor. At five, he goes home and thinks, "What a crappy day."

The next morning, the entrepreneur comes into work a bit earlier and carries an extra coffee. Before the other staff arrives, the boss makes more solid moves: approving yesterday's art, responding to a partnership offer, and scheduling two new clients. He's off to a great start.

Then the staff arrives and says, "The copier is out of ink."

The entrepreneur disengages from the valuable work—work that generates $500 per hour—and drives to the ink store, texts back and forth with the office staff to figure out which ink cartridge to buy, and drives back.

An hour later, the printer is working, but the owner is not.

Do you know what I think when I see a business owner burning his valuable time on small tasks? That farmer thinks he's a founder.

Your Kingmaker goal in the Farmer phase is an effective hourly rate of $50 per hour.

Take a look at your Roles and Tasks sheet (as a farmer, you should be filling it out each year) and note where you can be replaced for less than $50 per hour. Then do it. Replace yourself in those roles and get to work on higher-value tasks that create more than $50 an hour for the business. No more toilet-plunging!

SOLVE THE PROBLEMS THAT PULL YOU BACKWARD

After the founder has moved from working IN the business to working ON the business, his first question might be, "Now what?" but it should really be, "What have I missed?" When you cut yourself loose from those sub-$50-per-hour roles, you need to ensure that those jobs are getting done— and that they're getting done *right*—before you swing your attention to something new. Otherwise, you'll find yourself using your $50 hours to unclog the toilet.

Here's an example.

Alise runs a cookie delivery business in North Carolina, serving up fresh-baked goods and coffee to individual and corporate clients. She self-identifies as a "farmer" and has tried to cut back her hours, but she hasn't yet replaced herself in the sales role. So when she recently took time off to visit her parents in California, revenue plummeted. Alise scrambled back into the sales seat and was able to right the ship, but unfortunately, she's now convinced that the business can't run without her and will think twice before ever taking time away again.

She's wrong, of course. Her mistake wasn't to take time off to see her family; it was to take time off without handing the sales job over to someone on her team. Alise abdicated responsibility instead of delegating tasks.

Here's another example.

Russell owns a bakery in upstate New York and decided to boost his revenue with a Facebook ad campaign. It took him weeks to set up, and he spent much of his time closely monitoring ad spending and placement every day. This work is necessary, but it pulled him away from other places, namely his bakery counter. He doesn't greet clients every morning anymore. He's replaced himself with a minimum-wage teenager who doesn't like being awake at 6 a.m. to sell crullers and Danishes. His regular clients started to miss him, and then they started to leave.

Russell's influx of new clients was nice but fleeting. They'd show up once and never come back because an apple turnover is just a rare treat for them (and they don't really like the teenager at the front counter either). Russell jumped to marketing strategy before replacing himself with the right person in an essential client-facing role. He went after the "quick money" and lost his base.

One step forward, one step back: that's no way to run a business. And you know that. Until you solve the problems that pull you backward, your march forward will look like a salsa dance: fast-moving feet, smiling face, body going nowhere.

If you don't tell your staff exactly how to sweep the floors, they'll never do it the way you would. That means you'll spend too much time checking the floors instead of building a retention plan. And without a retention plan, your clients will leave too early, so you'll need to sell far more often to less-perfect clients. And without perfect clients, you'll have to work harder for less, which narrows your margins. Without good margins, you can't hire staff, and you're back to sweeping the floors yourself. It's the death spiral for many founders, and it will continue until they interrupt it with meaningful action in the proper steps.

Before jumping ahead from one stage of entrepreneurialism to the next, you must completely replace yourself at your current stage. You must solve the founder problems before tackling farmer problems. Don't plant seeds until the ground is fertile.

THE FARMER'S INCOME GOAL

In this section, you'll read about *The Pumpkin Plan* by Mike Michalowicz. It's required reading for everyone I coach. But Michalowicz's real work of genius is another book called *Profit First*.

THE PROFIT-FIRST MINDSET

"Profit First" isn't a woo-woo strategy of making wishes or "putting it out to the universe to provide." It's simply a matter of priority. We do things that are urgent instead of things that are important, and we value our debts to others over our own well-being. Michalowicz's book goes into great depth on the subject, and his strategy is more precise than my own. At Two-Brain Business, we teach Profit First a different way, depending on whether the entrepreneur is in the founder, farmer, or Tinker phase. Here are your primary goals in the Farmer phase:

- Achieve a 33 percent gross profit margin (which

includes your pay, through salaries or bonuses or other payouts).

- Control fixed costs and staff costs to achieve 33 percent.
- Pay yourself FIRST so expenses don't "creep up" and eat the profit margin.

In the Founder phase, the strategy of paying yourself at least $100 per week wasn't just to ensure you could eat; it was also to establish the habit of self-payment. In the Farmer phase, the habit can stay the same, but your self-payment should grow. Write yourself paychecks for the first and fifteenth of the month. Write them out in advance, six months at a time. Put the checks in an envelope, and take them to your bank for deposit. If possible, deposit these checks to a different bank than the one you use for the business so you can't easily transfer back and forth to feed the business with your grocery money. Now the money has been set aside.

Your secondary goals are:

- Keep staff costs to 44 percent of gross revenues or below (the 4/9 model I describe in a few pages).
- Keep fixed costs (rent, power, internet, insurance) to 22 percent of gross revenue or less.

The first step in growing a resilient business, impervious to corporate competition and burnout, is to identify your best clients. The second is to diversify your revenue streams based on what THEY want.

THE PATH TO PROFIT

What did your business look like five years ago? Probably not the same as it does today. Your services are probably different. If you sell a product, you're definitely selling a different product than you were five years ago. Want proof? Look around for a TV store or stereo shop. They're gone. The best businesses update their services or products to match the times, but your platform—your brand, your building, and your staff—can remain the same.

Three years ago, I went to visit Joel Salatin (author of *Folks, This Ain't Normal*) at his farm in Virginia. Joel's farm is named "Polyface Farm: The Farm of Many Faces" because Joel understands that his farm is a platform.

My phone's map couldn't even find Joel's farm. Thankfully, a neighbor gave me directions, and my rental car bumped along his long driveway at 8 a.m., a full hour before my farm tour was scheduled to start. I imagined a warm welcome from the "lunatic farmer" (Joel's self-given nickname) himself, catching the family at breakfast and enjoying a one-on-one interview before we toured the back forty. Instead, I was the third car to arrive. By 9 a.m., there were fifty people seated on Joel's hay wagon and fifty more on another wagon pulled by Joel's son. Each of us paid to be there.

The wagon lurched forward, pulled by a newish tractor, just as the Virginia skies opened up and drenched us with a driving rain—perfect weather for our first stop: Joel's pig corral.

Joel doesn't own a sty. He shelters his pigs in the forest, where they can root around like they would in the wild. He has impermanent fences everywhere and moves them every few days. Pig farms stink, but pigs that roam around in the forest—even in the rain—were almost stink-free. (Lucky for us.)

Joel's sustainable farming practices, like this one, were the primary attraction for most others on the wagon. His animals aren't confined to one fixed address, and all of his cages move. Cattle wander through rotating pastures; then, when they're moved a few days later, portable chicken coops take their spot. The chickens dig into the cow manure for worms, which tills the manure deep into the soil. It also makes for larger, healthier-looking chickens that live in the green grass instead of drawers. Joel's farm is full of cycles like these, epiphanies for the small farmer. Joel's operating system is a constant rotation of mini-ecological cycles of animal and vegetable. It's pretty cool, but that's not why I was there.

I was there to see Joel's platform.

Polyface Farm has multiple revenue streams.

His vegetables and meat sell at a local roadside stand. I saw constant traffic to the stand, but I see the same at Mennonite stands near my home. That's where most small-time farmers make most of their money.

On his 600-acre farm, Joel raises meat birds to sell to local restaurants. When his margins were disappearing because of increasing costs at the slaughterhouse, he opened his own slaughterhouse on his property. That's another revenue source. Local farmers bring their chickens to Joel to be slaughtered.

The same thing happened with beef. Joel raises beef cows. When abattoir costs rose, he opened an abattoir on his farm. Other farms bring their cows to Joel. That's another revenue stream.

Joel raises some chickens to lay eggs. He sells his eggs locally but also ships them out. That requires an egg packing and shipping business. Joel owns that, and other local farmers pay him to do it for them too.

He runs a farmer-internship program, where other farmers can live in trailers on his property and work for the summer. People pay him to do it. He has a waiting list and no labor costs.

One of his kids started an egg incubation business. Another started a company to raise chicks through adolescence. There are resale markets for chickens at each stage of their lives.

Another of his kids organizes school tours on the farm and charges for them.

Another has a dog breeding and grooming business, which provides the big dogs that keep Joel's animals safe.

And Joel frequently buys neighboring farms. Then he leases them to other farmers or keeps them under his own umbrella, rotating crops and animals on a larger scale through his valley.

Most small farmers are gone. Joel's farm is thriving because he sees it as a platform. Layer upon layer of services combine to build a resilient business. Cows graze and poop. Chickens till the manure into the soil. Crops grow faster because of the more fertile earth. Joel goes on frequent speaking tours, and people come to visit—hundreds every single day.

The key is to have a solid platform with flexible services.

When an audience changes (or even disappears), the platform can serve a new audience. No one wants to buy VCRs anymore, but the audience is still around. They just want different things now. VCR stores don't need to close; they just need to pivot on their platform.

When I opened my second gym, I thought I would keep my two businesses (personal training and CrossFit) separate. That decision doubled my costs and erected a barrier between two client audiences instead of capitalizing on the natural overlap. Only after a few years of juggling did I combine the two, and I immediately saw the benefit: the whole is more than the sum of its parts.

Since then, my gym has hosted birthday parties and feasts. I've done escape room challenges there and Ninja Warrior courses. Even my core services have expanded to include nutrition consultation and cognitive training. And if all else fails, I could revert to the auto body shop that used to occupy the space.

When the beef market takes a downturn, Joel Salatin is okay. He waits and sells more chickens. His view of the farm as a platform for general business instead of a niche for specialization makes him so resilient. When other farms fail, Joel grows. When other farmers seek answers, Joel does another speaking tour (or writes another book). And when a member of his staff wants to start a service of her own, Joel makes space for it under the Polyface umbrella.

For example, Joel isn't going to start a dog breeding service, but his platform creates both the opportunity and some demand for the service. We call this strategy "intrapreneurialism," establishing a platform for your staff to build their own "book of business" under your banner.

THE INTRAPRENEUR

An intrapreneurial relationship offers benefits to both sides. The farmer provides:

- An established brand
- Access to his client base
- Insurance
- A payment gateway
- Access to space
- Power, Wi-Fi, phone, and toilets
- A shortcut to starting a business
- Playbooks, contracts, and legal documents
- Access to his professional supporters (lawyers, accountants, etc.)
- Access to equipment
- Mentorship

The intrapreneurial staff person:

- Shows up on time
- Delivers the service to the farmer's standard

For this, the staffer collects up to 44 percent of the gross revenue generated by their service. We sometimes refer to this as the "4/9 model" because the owner starts to create a 33 percent profit margin by keeping his staff costs to 44 percent (4/9) or less.

The farmer benefits from creating intrapreneurial opportunities for two reasons.

First, new streams of revenue make the business less fragile. When the hens have a bad month, the farmer is still collecting rent from the beef business. Each small activity on the farm is less averse to short-term risk because of the larger platform. Of course, when all of the activities on the platform are working well, the farmer makes more money.

Second, the farmer's employees are more likely to stay when they feel control over their own destiny. The common threads to staff retention are continuing education, opportunity to control their future, and enough income to cover their needs (and a few wants). Many people want to feel entrepreneurial, but can't take the risks the farmer already has. If they're given intrapreneurial opportunities to build their own idea, they can feel like an entrepreneur under the farmer's umbrella, benefiting from his platform and being shielded from most risk.

So where do intrapreneurial opportunities come from? Interviews with your best clients. When asked, "What's your biggest challenge in life outside my doors?" your client will likely share a problem to which you can provide a solution. For example, many of my fitness clients would say, "Chris, the workouts are great, but when I leave the gym, I have an hour to get my kids fed, dressed, and across town to the soccer field. I usually have to grab takeout for all of us. My diet stinks!"

Of course, this offers me the perfect opportunity for a meal-preparation or delivery service or a partnership with a local restaurant. It could also create an intrapreneurial opportunity for someone on my team: a trainer at the gym could teach our clients how to prepare food in advance.

The purpose of creating intrapreneurial opportunities is to help your staff build meaningful careers in your business. But keep in mind that everything the staff person does will be associated with your brand, so it's essential that they deliver to your gold standard.

After determining which new service to offer, you should be the first to perform it for the first client, leaving tracks as you go. Write down the standard operating procedures, any mistakes or gaps you discover, and define the gold standard for delivery. Then, after the first client, hand off the service to a staff member after training them how to deliver top value. Then, after a few months, evaluate the staff member to ensure their delivery meets your own.

INCREASING YOUR SERVICES AND PACKAGES

What are the three primary services you sell?

Mastery of those three is critical before you branch out and diversify. All possible combinations of those three services should be exhausted before adding a fourth. However, when these criteria are met and...

1. a client tells you that she NEEDS more help
2. a staff person has the bandwidth and passion for running the new thing
3. there's a clear path to profit

...then it's time to diversify. This is part of what makes you a farmer, after all.

Looking back on Salatin's farm as a "platform" for services, what are the opportunities in your business? What is the "low-hanging fruit" that would be quick to add, easy to implement, an obvious win for your clients, AND won't just buy you another job?

Choose one idea, and put the others on hold—for now. You can always do them later. As you'll read in the Tinker section, having too many ideas is the curse of the entrepreneur. Then talk to the staff member who will serve as the primary intrapreneur for the new service. Then clearly delineate the most basic version of the service. You don't need to explore all options, bells, and whistles yet. Just determine a minimum viable product.

Next, determine the time required to deliver the service. Price the service according to the time required for delivery. Remember to always be increasing the value of your time. Finally, launch the service with your primary clients first, and get their feedback. For example, Shawn runs a gym in Massachusetts and decided it was time to add a specialty program for people looking to run their first 5K.

The first question he asked was: "Which of my coaches has the time, expertise, and passion for running the program?" Then he brought up the idea with the best coach for the job. They discussed how the specialty program would fit into the coach's growth plan and how she stood to benefit as an intrapreneur. Next, Shawn considered how a running program might impact his current offerings. Would some of his gym members quit and do the running program as a replacement, resulting in a net loss of revenue? Or would they add it on to their current workouts?

To make sure his coach was also increasing the value of her time and energy, Shawn set a price slightly higher than his other programs. Finally, the course launched to the members of his gym first, then to their friends, next to the gym's partners, and finally to the community at large. Notice that the primary services offered at Shawn's gym (personal training, nutrition, and CrossFit classes) weren't negatively impacted by the addition of the fourth service. Also, as a farmer, Shawn protected his time instead of just adding more work to his overfilled plate. Most importantly, the path to profit was clear.

Intrapreneurialism is a great way to expand, strengthen, and diversify your platform and revenue streams. But there is something else happening here. Did you spot it? In delegating entire services to someone on your team, you're making the crucial shift from delivery to management and reducing the time you spend in the varied corners of your business. You're taking back your time, and it's one of the most important elements of the Farmer phase.

THE FARMER'S TIME GOAL

In the Founder phase, you measured your Effective

Hourly Rate (EHR) to determine the value of your time. One of the first ways to increase the value of that time is to decrease the time you actually spend working. Your goal in the Farmer phase is to decrease your workload to forty quality hours per week. It is a positive constraint that forces you to focus on *valuable* tasks instead of being sucked down the rabbit hole of social media or merely tending the fires.

Like expenses to revenue, your work will always expand to fill the time you have. If you budget seventy hours per week, you'll be busy for seventy hours per week, but that's not to say you'll be productive for those seventy hours. At best, each of us spends two to four hours at our peak "flow" state and another two to four hours in a state of "pretty good." After four hours, our judgment is impaired by fatigue. After eight hours, we're a danger to our business. Go home!

The most important measure of your value to the company is your EHR. Is it going up? Are you becoming a more valuable leader? Or is it going down? Are you being sucked into the wrong work?

CASE STUDY: THE HANDYMAN

"I'm working my tail off. All of my employees are making more money, but I'm not." Randy is a handyman. He can fix plumbing. He can rough-in electrical work, frame walls, repair roofs, and install windows. But Randy's specialty is building decks on houses. He makes beautiful, sturdy decks. He also maintains pools for a growing number of his clients. Every year in the spring, Randy backs up with work. Clients want their pools cleaned and filled, they want their decks stained or braced, and they might ask him to take down a dead tree or do some other maintenance "while he's at it." Randy has more work than he can handle, and he knows it.

Two years ago, Randy hired a couple of other handymen to help him. One is still with him, and the other was a slacker who required constant oversight. In conversation with Randy, he outlined his problems:

> "I hate to keep people waiting, but every time I build a new deck on a client's house, their neighbor asks me to build a deck for them. And then they ask me to do a bunch of other stuff while I'm at their house. My clients keep waiting longer and longer, but I can't find good people to work for me. My clients want to see ME at their house, and besides, no one does it as well as I do."

After speaking with Randy for a half hour, I identified a few other problems:

- As Randy's client list gets longer, his best clients will

eventually tire of waiting for their pools to be ready in the spring and start to look for help elsewhere.

- As his long-term clients leave, Randy will become more and more dependent on finding new ones. The new clients will likely be less loyal, and that cycle will continue to speed up.
- Randy's missing easy opportunities to serve his clients more ("Why don't I have your lawn trimmed while I'm here?") because he doesn't have time.
- Randy's doing work far below his value. Painting a deck can be done by a low-skilled worker, but plumbing can't.

Randy's staff can only make more money by working more hours. They're going to either leave or become unmotivated if he doesn't grow his business.

Finally, when a new client orders a pool, Randy immediately buys it and stores it even if he can't get to the job for a couple of months. This places an enormous burden on his cash flow while he stores the supplies. If he buys the pool for $5,000 on June 1 and can't install it until August 1, he's out the money for two months. And what if the customer doesn't pay him right away? Worse, what if the client says, "Oh, I don't want that anymore"? It's scary even to consider, but it happens to Randy at least once per year. He has a "hot tub graveyard" behind his overstuffed garage.

Randy has bought himself a job. He's making some money and has one dependable staff person, but he's still working far too hard and doing low-level work. He doesn't have any idea how to get out of his position unless he can find someone else, "but good people cost money that I don't have." Randy's job as a handyman is thriving, but as an entrepreneur, he's struggling in the Farmer phase.

I asked Randy, "Do you want to have a business and employ people, or do you want to stay this busy yourself but make more money?"

He took his time and thought about it. Most people don't. But Randy is over forty now, and thinking about retirement. "I want to work less and make more money," he said. He was kind of shy about it, as though there's anything wrong with working less and earning what you're worth.

I nodded my head and said, "Let's begin."

The first step in Randy's journey to a successful business is to break down all of the roles and tasks in his business. For example:

- Painter
- Carpenter
- Plumber

- Lawn care
- Pool cleaner
- Pool installer
- Bookkeeper/collections
- Sales
- Foreman

We found around ten more when we really dug in.

Next, I had Randy write a job description for each role (it wasn't his favorite exercise). When we pored over the tasks required to fulfill each position, I asked Randy, "What do you think that person should be paid?"

"Well," he said, looking at the lawn care role, "I usually just end up cutting the grass myself, since I'm at the house installing the deck anyway. But when I look at this list, it seems obvious that a high school kid could do it." We set the "lawn care" pay rate of $12.50 per hour—slightly more than minimum wage. Then we moved on to the painter role. Randy said the skill required was slightly higher than lawn care, so I suggested a rate of $18 per hour. He agreed, but said, "Good luck getting a painter to work for eighteen bucks an hour."

So we pulled up the task list of the painter again. Randy really needed someone to stain decks and maybe do some exterior trim work. He wasn't doing the highly skilled work of a professional interior painter. I said, "Given the work you're doing, do you need a pro?"

"No," he answered. "I guess I could teach someone to stain decks and paint trim. Those are easy. And if you make a mistake, no one will know about it."

Then I asked if the opportunity to paint the interior of houses ever came up.

"Yeah, all the time," he said. "When I put in a pool, people usually want me to install a sliding glass door in their wall so they can see it. So I have to reframe the wall, then install the door. Most of the time, they want to change the color of the wall too. So that takes me a day to set up and paint."

I suggested he outsource the painting to a partner. "Know any good pros?"

"Oh yeah," he said. "I run into them at the hardware store all the time when I go pick up supplies."

First, I added "supplies purchaser" to his list of roles. Then I asked, "If you called those painters and offered to give them your interior paint work for a 10 percent commission, do you think they'd go for it?"

"In a heartbeat!" he answered. "They'd still keep around nine hundred bucks to paint the wall. Or they'd just mark up the job to cover my hundred bucks commission."

So we worked out what Randy actually made when he painted a wall. After supplies, it came to around $200, but it burned up a whole day. That meant Randy was making about $13 per hour of painting if we didn't include runs to the hardware store and prep time.

"That's barely more than my new imaginary lawn boy!" he laughed. But he didn't smile for long. He was starting to get it. The point we were working toward was establishing the value of Randy's time. He saw cash coming in and money going out, but he wasn't thinking about the investment of his time.

We moved on to the sales role. "If you actually answered your phone, took down payments, and then assigned the work out, how many more jobs could you take?" I asked.

"None," he said. "I don't have the staff."

"If you did have the staff," I poked again, "how many more jobs could you take?"

"Oh, tons," he replied. "I just took my ad out of the newspaper because we have too much work."

Then I asked, "If you were ONLY taking orders and collecting checks, how many hours per week would that take?"

He laughed. "Yeah, I wish. That would take maybe twenty hours per week."

I followed with an emotional jab: "What would that mean to your family, to have you working twenty hours per week?"

Randy was taken aback. He'd never considered it. His entire sense of self-worth was wrapped up in being "a hard worker" and a "good provider." He'd entered the martyrdom mindset, and it was hurting his family. Last year, he didn't make a single baseball game and usually skipped the weekend birthday parties and barbecues. I knew his wife was tired of apologizing for him and turning up on her own. And his kids were getting older too. They didn't have many summers left at home.

"Randy," I said, "it's time to stop being a martyr. Who is the easiest person to hire on this list?"

He said, immediately, "The lawn care person. My nephew is a teenager. He's looking for work. But he doesn't have any handyman skills, so I thought I didn't have anything for him."

We agreed that Randy's strategy for the next two months would be:

- Hire his nephew at $12.50 per hour, plus gas.
- Reinvest the time Randy usually spends mowing lawns (around five hours per week) into calling current clients and asking if they'd like their yards mowed. Fill the lawn mower's schedule first. With five hours to spend calling clients, Randy was confident he could fill the kid's schedule.
- When his schedule is full, hire a painter for decks and trim. Randy (or his handyman assistant) was spending around eight hours per week on this role. Pay the painter $18 per hour and shift the handyman assistant into more of Randy's higher-value work, then move Randy into filling the next position.

It's true: Randy's pretty hard to replace. Almost no one has his combined skillset in plumbing, deck building, lawn mowing, painting, pool installation, and all the other stuff. But many people have one or two of those skills (and some are even better than he is). They won't be as fast, but they'll please the clients. It will still be hard to hire another handyman, but that's okay. Randy's excellent assistant can also be moved to higher-value work as his lower-value roles are backfilled. That will make him happier. It will also potentially create a foreman role for him in the future, as Randy continues to climb the ladder we're building.

Our first calculation, replacing Randy in just the lawn care and painting roles, cut nearly a week off his wait time for his current clients and generated $800 per week in NET revenue to Randy's company. It's just the first steps, but Randy has more energy at our meetings now. He's becoming a true entrepreneur.

THE FARMER'S BRAND

In the Farmer phase, the team becomes the brand. As a farmer, you must now take the business's brand from "me" to "we" by consciously referring to "the team" or "us" instead of saying "my" or "mine." For example, an insurance company should stop saying "Chris, the broker" and start saying "the team at Super Broker Brothers."

Some brands, like Zappos, do such a fantastic job of building the team culture that clients actually want to work with the company because they know the team is happy. That's the gold standard, but as a farmer, you should first concern yourself with solving the "icon problem."

REPLACING YOURSELF: SOLVING THE "ICON PROBLEM"

The first hurdle in replacing yourself in any role is to solve the icon problem. As the figurehead for your business, clients expect to see you in every position and view your staff only as substitutes of lesser value. For example:

- Athletes ask which classes you'll be coaching and book around those times.
- Clients aren't willing to do some of their training sessions with another trainer.
- "When will Chris be back?" is a common question in the gym.
- Members text you, saying, "It's not the same when you're not here."

These are flattering at first. You feel loved and irreplaceable. But don't fall into the trap. How will you ever take a week off without your business struggling? How can you ever sell your gym or move on to a higher-value role or make the time to improve your business? If clients are disappointed when you're not around all the time, you're an icon. That's a problem.

"My clients think I'm their personal servant!" Have you heard that one before?

"They think I can just drop everything and listen to their little dramas!" I've been there.

"They think I just drink coffee and surf the internet when I'm not coaching!" Been there too.

When I finally realized that a stable income meant working ON my business, not IN it, I struggled to separate myself from the day-to-day stuff. I wrote blog posts and read articles while sitting at the front desk of my gym. Clients felt like I was ignoring them. When I expanded and put in a small office, they'd knock and ask why I was "hiding" in there. I was frustrated because I really liked these people and didn't want them to think I was avoiding them, but I also needed to get things done, or the gym would fail. It took a long time to realize they were knocking on my door because they didn't know other coaches could answer their question.

The only replacement for an icon is a team. Establish the expertise and authority of your staff. Refer to yourself as one of "the team." Attend seminars led by your stylists. Attend your coaches' classes as an athlete. Take yourself off the pedestal. And when you remove yourself from a role, hand it over completely and let everyone know.

I had a booming personal training business in 2012: thirty clients spent a minimum of one hour each week with me, and that revenue was a significant part of our business. It was a risk to stop taking one-on-one clients, but I knew the only way I could devote the time necessary to create a sustainable business was to cut back. I just didn't have any other time. It was scary to hand clients off to another trainer, but I started to identify a few who might make the switch. I told them the change was absolutely necessary and that I'd miss training them, and I assured them they would be in good hands. Unfortunately, I forgot one detail:

"Why can you train HER but not ME?"

I couldn't pick and choose a smaller clientele because someone's feelings would be hurt. Because of my own "icon problem," I had to remove myself from personal training. I had to establish the expertise of my other coaches quickly and then stop doing one-on-one training entirely. You can avoid this problem by demonstrating the expertise of your replacements *before* you step back. If your coaches want a career in fitness, they can have it, and you can help by creating intrapreneurial opportunities and then backing away.

THE FARMER'S MARKETING PLAN

In the Founder phase, I introduced the Affinity Marketing strategy. We placed the founder at the center of the bull's-eye and practiced Affinity Marketing on her personal connections.

Now, in the Farmer phase, we start by identifying your best clients and then determining how your service can help their loved ones (Affection Loop), coworkers or buddies (Activity Loop), and people with similar habits (Acquaintance Loop). Finally, we start the process of marketing to strangers: working on the Attention and Audiences Loops.

This is a long section, but since we're building your sales and marketing strategy, it's an important one. I recommend you download the Affinity Marketing Cheat Sheet from the Founder section (or from TwoBrain.com/affinity) and work through it with some of your *best* clients. I emphasize working with your best clients because those are the only opinions that matter. It's time to talk about your seed clients and your weed clients.

HOW TO GROW PERFECT APPLES

I grew up with apples.

St. Joseph Island, situated on Lake Huron, is home to hundreds of family farms, and every one of them has an orchard. In the late 1800s, a packing plant collected and shipped the apples, but it's long gone. Its legacy is hundreds of small orchards scattered across the island. Many have gone wild. All have cross-pollinated, creating varieties of apples that don't exist anywhere else.

When you cross-pollinate two apple trees, you get a new type of apple. Those apples drop seeds, which grow into trees. Over generations, new types of apples are born, and old varieties disappear. Apples are an excellent metaphor for business—and life. This story is about one particular tree and what it taught me about quality.

Outside the front window of our family home grew a yellow melba, a particularly crunchy variety of apple with very thin skin. As a kid, I thought the tree was a type of Granny Smith because the apples grew green until the very last moment when they'd pale to yellow and then drop, ready for eating. They had a loud crunch and a tang that would have made a great cider. All in all, a great apple tree for a family: you could eat them off the branch, cook them in a pie, or even press them for juice. You can imagine my panic when a guy showed up with a chainsaw and headed straight for the tree.

An apple tree is many things—provider of food, shelter of birds, and great curb appeal—but it's never been much of a defender against a chainsaw. Ten minutes after his arrival, the woodcutter had most of the tree on the ground: whole limbs, all of the leaves, and almost all of the branches. The tree looked dead. I have only a few traumatic memories from my teen years, but that tree was one. And there's no reasoning with a teenager, so when my dad explained what "pruning" meant, I didn't listen. I raged about it and then sulked for days. Of course, the next year, the tree came back far healthier than before.

With the dead weight gone, the good branches got all of the tree's water and nutrients and bore bigger, sweeter fruit.

What every farmer knows—and I didn't know then—was that a tree will try to feed a dead branch. It will pour energy, water, and nutrients into its weakest branches just as much as its best ones. And what happens next? The best branches are starved. They're limited in their ability to bear fruit.

The analogy is probably rising toward the surface, but it took years for me to link this lesson to my business. It wasn't until I read Mike Michalowicz's *The Pumpkin Plan* that I really understood: you pour time and energy into your clients, staff, and business processes. You spend as much time and energy on the poor ones as you do on the best, and that's harming your ability to provide the best service. For example, if you have five part-time staff members who are doing pretty good work, you could be preventing the hire of one incredible staff member who would do excellent work. If you have one client who sucks up all your time and energy, it's probably stopping you from allowing your better clients to become amazing clients because you don't have time to ask how you can serve them more.

My business mentor, Dan Martell, once told me, "It's different for every type of industry, but at the core, the team wants to do their best work, and you can't do that if you don't bring in the client who will allow the best work to be done." And if you have one time-sucking process, like updating your website, you could waste hours trying to fix your blog, or you could spend those same hours meeting people who might like your service.

Early in my career as a personal trainer, I had a client who drained me emotionally. Her name was Sharon, and I would dread her Tuesday morning appointments. All day Monday, I'd be distracted while I thought about her mental state the next day. On Tuesday, I'd carry a high heart rate while I prayed she'd cancel. After her appointment, when Sharon finally left the building, I'd be so emotionally exhausted that my level of care suffered for all my other clients. Sharon would negatively affect the experiences of dozens of other clients. Many of those clients were excellent. And one of them probably would have scooped up her appointment time if it were available. But I clung to Sharon for years, because I thought it was wrong to fire a client, just like I thought it was wrong to prune a tree.

A tree needs air, light, water, and food. Your business needs leadership, inspiration, staff, and cash flow. All of those resources are finite. If you give a share of the water to a dead branch, the best branches can't bear fruit. It's tempting, as a founder, to spend all your time planting seeds. If you're like me, you probably have a pocket full of them. Maybe you have fertile ground and a barrel of rainwater. But your time is often best spent pruning what you have instead of planting what you don't. The first step in focusing on your fruit-bearing branches is to identify them.

Not every client deserves the same attention. A client might always be right, but they're not always equal. I interviewed Mike Michalowicz and asked him about the hierarchy of clients. He said,

> "There are three types of clients. There are good clients, there are bad clients, and then there's no client. A good client is best. We all know that. But we think a bad client is second best, and the worst client is no client because there's no revenue. I found the reality is actually this: the best client is the good client, the second-best client is no client at all, and a bad client is actually the worst."

The "squeaky wheels" often drown out the voices of your best. Trying to please two hundred cranky clients is like herding cats, whereas duplicating and growing your best clients creates a quiet, happy garden.

Another reason to focus on your BEST clients is their Net Promoter Score. I won't break down the whole scale here, but let's imagine you ranked your clients on a scale of 1 to 10, where a 10 meant they were extremely likely to recommend you to their friends. A 1, of course, would mean that they're probably bad-mouthing you to their friends, and a 5 is neutral. It's much easier to make a 5 into an 8 than it is to turn a 1 into a 5. For example, it's easier to delight a mediocre client, turning them into an evangelist for your service than it is to change the mind of someone who dislikes your service. And even if you DO fix the 1 client, you'll only move them up to neutral: satisfied but still not talking about you.

Here is a hacked version of an exercise in Mike Michalowicz's *The Pumpkin Plan* to determine your best clients:

1. Make two lists.
2. On the first list, record your top ten clients by the amount they pay you. This is the "money" list.
3. On the second list, record your top ten clients by how happy they make you. This is the "joy" list.
4. Now compare the "money" and "joy" lists side-by-side. Which names appear on both? These are your seed clients, according to Michalowicz.

Next, you'll want to hear—in THEIR words—why they're using your service. Set up interviews with each seed client individually. Ask them:

- "What do you like most about my haircuts?"
- "What frustrates you most about getting a haircut in general?"
- "What's your biggest source of stress when you leave my salon?"

The answers to these questions will tell you:

- What your most prominent marketing message should be.
- What you should fix or avoid doing altogether.
- Other opportunities to help your clients, partner with other professionals, or generate revenue.

Let's say a regular client makes an appointment for a haircut at the Side Hustle Salon. After their appointment, the two of you go to the coffee shop down the street and grab a table. Over coffee, you work the three questions above into your conversation. Your client answers:

"I like the informal attitude and the fact I can get in on weekends."

"The worst part is maintaining my cut after I get home. I always seem to get frizzy in a couple of days."

"My biggest source of stress is definitely my kids, especially on weekends when they have nothing to do."

Bingo. First, you should be promoting the fact that you're open on weekends to everyone who will listen. Second, you should keep a few hair products on hand that will help your clients maintain their cuts, or at least allow them to order products through your site. Third, you should consider partnering with a local kids' activity: parents can make an appointment to drop their kids at the Lego center and tick a box to book an appointment with you at the same time automatically. Then, after you've cut their hair, they shuttle the kids in one at a time.

Here's an example from my first gym. I believed my seed clients came to my gym because the workouts were intense, the coaching was technical, and the community felt like friends. But when I interviewed my seed clients, their answers surprised me. They said:

> "I don't have to think when I'm at your gym." (We're a coaching facility, not an access facility.)

> "I always feel happier when I leave than I did when I got there."

> "This is the only place where people tell me I'm doing a good job."

Obviously, that insight was different from what I had anticipated. I immediately changed our brand to "The

Happy Gym" on my billboards and website. I started writing more content about how exercising in a group, under the watchful eye of a coach, makes you happier. And I focused on delighting my seed clients instead of patching up the little problems my less-than-perfect-fits complained about.

My next task was to increase the value of my seed clients. During one interview, a seed client said, "Chris, when I leave the gym, it's 6 p.m. My kids have to get to baseball practice before seven. Dinner isn't made yet. So most of the time I go through a drive-thru to pick up dinner. I know it's probably canceling out the work I do in the gym, but it's the only way I can get here every day."

I asked myself, "What if the gym had a nutrition program or partnership with a food-delivery service? What if the gym sold ready-made meals or organized client meal-swaps on the weekends? Or what if we partnered with a local grocery store to set up curbside pickup?" Meijer does it for free already. Guess what happened? My best clients were delighted. My worst clients complained about the cost and didn't use the service. My mediocre clients moved up a few notches on the Net Promoter Score and became brand evangelists.

The reason we call your best clients the Axial Loop is that your business revolves around them. Your service is not the sun at the center of the universe; your best clients are the sun, and your service revolves around them. If I discovered that nutrition coaching would help my clients more than fitness coaching, I'd set up a nutrition business with a squat rack in the back parking lot.

The next step is to identify your dead branches. What if you could trade your five worst clients for five more of your BEST clients? When I interviewed Michalowicz, he also talked about what do with your WORST clients: "It sounds bold, but fire those bottom feeders because the 'revenue' you lose is so insignificant compared to the opportunity to gain more great clients."

If you're like me, that phrase ("worst clients") sends a shiver up your spine. The client is always right, aren't they? Don't we need to latch onto every client we can possibly get? But let's say you could trade your worst clients for better ones, Who would you swap? If you're like me, it didn't take you long to come up with your answer.

There's value in knowing who your best clients are—and who they're not. Because when we identify where best clients come from, what they want, and why they stay, we attract more clients like them. And when we identify the same characteristics of our worst clients, we avoid painful mistakes in the future. Let's redo the Apples exercise, this time with your top-secret list of worst clients. We'll call it the "Weeds" exercise.

1. Make two lists.
2. On the first list, write down the people who pay the least for your services. Calculate this by dividing their monthly rate by their average visits. No judgment here, we just want to know who pays the least per visit.
3. On the second list, note who complains most. Who makes your energy drop when they walk through the door?
4. Now compare the two lists. Which names appear on both?

Michalowicz would have you fire those clients immediately, but if that's uncomfortable for you, that's okay. When you start improving your service offerings, they'll probably leave anyway. Ask yourself what these "weed" clients have in common:

· Where did they come from?
· How much do they pay?
· What are their requests?
· How are these answers different from your seed clients?

If all of your "worst clients" came from six-week challenges, consider forgoing more six-week challenges. If all of your "squeaky wheels" are currently paying at a discounted rate, consider eliminating discounts. If your most disruptive clients are likely to quit if you raise your rates, consider making the same money with fewer people. Then raise your prices.

Mike Michalowicz points out: "A lot of people measure the quality client by their words, but I argue we should measure the quality of the client by their wallets." I agree with him. You don't need everyone. If you ask yourself, "How did I get this client?" for both your apples and your weeds, you can start trading worst for best by modifying your own behaviors. Stop doing the things that grow weeds and start planting more apple trees. Set a deadline to start making those "trades." What's your plan? Now comes the hard part: what do we do with the low-producing, barely living branches? The answer may surprise you.

INCREASING THE VALUE OF YOUR SERVICE

As you improve your service, its value will also increase. That means raising your rates, adding upgrades, or diversifying into new services. The more you increase the value of your service, the more you can charge for it, and the more you charge for it, the more likely it is that your weed clients will drop off on their own.

Before reading the rest of this section, it's important to

note that you must deliver your core products before branching off into new revenue streams. No one will order Uber Eats food delivery if they've just taken a ride in a dirty Uber, and no one buys expensive shampoo for a lousy haircut. In the Founder phase, we determined your core services for two reasons:

- To spend time working on what your clients actually want.
- To avoid wasting time on things your clients don't want.

Constant improvement to your service means a continuous increase in value. And that means constant upgrades in price. Nearly a third of all mentoring clients we serve at Two-Brain Business have had to go through a tough rate increase. They typically struggle because:

- The entrepreneur was projecting his own budget onto his clients and believed they couldn't afford the new rate.
- The entrepreneur waited too long, and his clients were anchored into the old price.

Both of those problems were solvable, but the emotional toll on the owner and client was higher than it had to be. The easy solution to solving both problems is to make automatic, incremental upgrades to your rate every year (like 3 percent, for example.) Then you announce your "2021 Rates" when necessary. But if you HAVE waited too long, there's a proven process to make a rate hike of 10 to 15 percent. We've used this strategy with hundreds of clients successfully. While the delivery might differ by industry, the approach is useful across the board.

Calculate how much each client SHOULD be paying to create your "perfect day." Base this calculation off 150 clients. More isn't better.

Determine a date for the change. You'll want to give members about ten days' notice: enough to be forewarned, too little to ruminate. Note: if you have a cancellation policy larger than ten days, you have to provide longer notice than the cancellation period. And if someone's on a long-term contract, you have to honor that contract. Good luck.

Spread the news. Post about the change on your blog, share on your FB page, and email to all members. Eliminate any possibility that a member won't find out. Delete those posts after the change occurs so future members don't see it.

Email the "worst offenders" personally. There should be fewer than ten here. Follow the same template, but add a dollar value: "Your discount has resulted in a savings of $830 per year, or $4150 since we moved out of my garage..."

Now, the tough part: overcoming YOUR fear. Most of the awkwardness, resistance, and anger you're picturing in your clientele are really just the fears you're projecting onto them. So we'll cut straight to the worst-case scenario.

WHAT'S THE WORST THAT COULD HAPPEN?

Calculate the projected gross revenues if a client moves to the new price without discounts. Let's say it's going to be 100 clients × $150 = $15,000.

Subtract your current gross revenues from that projection. Let's say it's 100 clients × an ARM of $125 currently ($12,500 total.) The difference is $2,500/month.

Divide that difference by the new membership rate. This will tell you how many clients you can lose and still make the same income (with fewer coaching hours, probably): $2,500/$150 (the new rate) = sixteen clients, for example.

Walk through your client list. Can you identify sixteen clients who will DEFINITELY quit when the rates go up? If not, you're crazy not to do this, especially if your business isn't providing you with a good living. Prepare yourself to lose those clients (but you probably won't).

Hit Send.

Call your mentor every few hours with updates. You'll want to have emotional backup, trust me.

I've been through this with many businesses now. The process gets more refined every time but NEVER comes close to reaching the "acceptable limits" for attrition. Usually one or two members will drag their heels because they're scared of change and might even quit. Some might come back. But keep this in mind: the clients, staff, and business required to get you to the "perfect day" is probably not the same one that got you to this point.

AFFINITY MARKETING IN THE FARMER STAGE

Your Affinity Marketing process will start with those apple clients. It's time to get them talking. When a client visits for coffee or a goal review session or an annual planning meeting, the first question to ask is: "Are you completely satisfied with your progress since our last meeting?"

If they say "Yes!" then make them famous.

Say, "I'm so pumped for you. I'd love to tell your story. I have a camera here on my phone, and I want you to say what you just said. Ready?" I've never had a single client—in any industry—turn down the opportunity to get featured or celebrated. After all, it's their favorite story!

Then ask the client, "Who's been most helpful to you in your progress?" You're really asking who their primary support comes from. Then offer to help THAT person. That's the person in your client's life with the highest affinity. It's probably someone in their family or their best friend. That person is in your client's first loop: Affection. How can your service help them solve their problem?

Next, look at the Affinity Marketing Cheat Sheet. Knowing what you do about the client, who else in their life could benefit from your service? Is it a coworker? A friend? Make a clear suggestion instead of asking a general question:

> "I know this is a busy time of year in your office. Do you think any of your coworkers are putting off their tax preparation until the last minute?"

Or,

> "I know the other teachers in your school are getting ready for the summer. They must be excited! Do you think any of them are trying to figure out how to fit into their swimsuit?"

Or (an easy one):

"I'm so excited for your wedding. It's going to be immaculate! Are any of the members of your wedding party getting married in the next twelve months?"

Then make a clear offer to help those people with your service. It becomes effortless with practice.

After exhausting the first three Affinity Loops (family, coworkers, and friends), your next most likely conversions will come from your email list. It comprises the people who are paying attention, even if they're not yet paying you money.

Only after you have exhausted these opportunities should you move from Affinity Marketing to build online sales funnels with Google, YouTube, Facebook, and the rest. You can read a more in-depth strategy, take a free course, and get the book for FREE at TwoBrain.com/affinity.

The Affinity Loops that sit at the far edge of the bull's-eye (Awareness, Audiences, and Ambient Loops) hold the people who have more than one degree of separation with your business. Social media, like Facebook; search engines, like Google; and other online marketing is mighty but continuously changing (and therefore not useful to describe in a printed book). If you download the free Affinity Marketing book from our site, you'll find updated best practices in those loops. And of course, our mentorship program teaches a very tactical, in-depth process for maximizing your marketing online.

SALES IN THE FARMER STAGE

Who is the person most likely to buy from you next month? It's the person already buying from you this month. The sales process doesn't end when a client signs on the dotted line. It doesn't stop after their first session. It doesn't end after their contract expires. It NEVER ends. Professional salesmen lean on the "ABC" principle (Always Be Closing). A farmer can take that motto to heart and repeat it every time his team serves a client. But many farmers prefer this slogan instead: "ABK" (Always Be Keeping).

RETENTION FIRST

Sales to your current clients can take two forms. The first is to increase the length of a client's engagement with your business (LEG). The second is to increase the client's recurring purchase value. (ARM. But you can also think of it as "Average Revenue per Member" or "Average Revenue per Visit.") Your average client's value is determined by multiplying those factors—LEG and ARM—together. In other words, take a client's average value per visit (or per month) and multiply it by the number of visits or months they use your service. In the next section, we'll build the ARM of your best clients. But first let's talk about retention strategy, specifically bright spots.

"Bright spots" is a behavioral modification strategy. I stole the idea from researchers at Carnegie Mellon and Harvard Universities (George Lowenstein, and Chip and Dan Heath, respectively) and tweaked it for business purposes. The first bright spots opportunity occurs at the conversion point. This is where we first meet the client and ask the most important question of all: "How can I help?"

What benefit does your client want? That's your starting point. Sell the benefits of your service, NOT the features. Don't just list a menu of what you're selling. Tell your clients what those services will do for them. For example, if a client wants to look professional for a job interview, he needs you to say, "You need a more conservative haircut and a shave." The alternative—telling a client, "I sell haircuts, trims, waxes, styles, perms, shaving, and coloring"—leaves him alone to connect the dots between what he wants and what you can sell him. He probably doesn't KNOW what he needs. You do.

First, the client has to trust your judgment. He must first decide you have his best interests in mind. He already knows what you KNOW. Now he needs to know that you CARE. So I start the process with a question: "How can I help?" When most service people ask this same question, they're really asking, "What do you want to buy?" But not me. I want to know how the client will view success. So I take notes as they're speaking to demonstrate how important their goals are to my recommendation. Consider the difference between these two questions:

- "What service do you want me to perform?"
- "What outcome will my service create for you?"

The second question is where the client begins to make an emotional connection to your service. If the gentleman preparing for a job interview can see himself getting the job after using your service, you'll create a stronger bond. So the first question necessary for behavior modification is: "What will success look like?" In other words, "If I do a great job on your hair, what will happen?" He'll impress his interviewer and get the job.

The second question in the behavioral modification process is: "Where is our starting line?" It's important for the client to know he's already doing something right, that he's not starting from ground zero. This creates momentum that will lead to fulfillment. In this case, the hairdresser might say, "You already have very clean and soft hair. What are you using for shampoo and conditioner?" Her praise will be the client's first Bright Spot, and start the foundation of trust. The praise must be genuine, and reinforce what the client is already doing well.

Next, the hairdresser makes a recommendation based on the client's goal (benefit of service) and bright spots (what they're currently doing.) She also sets the stage for retention by asking, "If this goes well, what kind of job are you hoping to get?" She can also help the client maintain their new look with a few tips before they leave. But the next step—the follow-up—will set the hairdresser apart from her competition.

After the client leaves the shop, the hairdresser can type a quick email: "Well? How did it go? Did you get the job?" and schedule it to send for a date after the client's job interview. This requires less than thirty seconds of work but will reinforce the level of trust and care between the two. When the client responds, he'll give either a positive "I got it!" or a negative "I didn't get it," which creates an opportunity either way.

In the first instance ("I got it!") the hairdresser can simply congratulate the client and include a booking link for his next appointment. In the second, the pro can offer her condolences and add, "Tell me all about it as soon as you can. Here's a link to my schedule. See you soon!" The client still knows their hairdresser cares and has a clear path to booking the next service.

Many hairdressers will say, "I don't have time for that!" and they're right. They need to replace themselves in a lower-value role to create the time to make sales.

In the gym, clients start with a conversation: What have you done before? What do you like? What do you hope to achieve? From there, goals can be split into small microgoals (bright spots) and attached to emotions. ("How will losing five pounds make you feel? How will others react? What's the first thing you'll notice?") Follow-up calls and emails reinforce client successes. When clients are successful, they want others to know. What good is a gold medal without a podium to stand triumphantly atop?

The second phase of bright spots is a process we call "goal review."

Every quarter, if possible, book an appointment with your client and review their goals with your service. Extend their regular appointment time by five minutes, or schedule a separate time. It will be tough to meet every client if you're selling bagels and coffee, of course, but could you meet with a few? Identify your best clients in the next section, and do goal review meetings with them. No matter your business, if you're in the service industry, a goal review session is a simple and important exercise.

First question: "Has your overall goal changed since you started/since our last goal review?"

Second question: "What is it now?"

Third question: "Are you happy with the progress you've made?"

Here's where it gets interesting: depending on the client's answer to the third question, you can take one of two paths.

Path 1: "I'm not satisfied with my progress." If your client says, "No, I wish I was making faster progress," it's time to introduce an objective measure. If you sell financial services, show the client a chart of her portfolio's growth. If you're selling nutrition services, show the client a chart of his weight loss progress. Then make a new prescription. Honestly ask yourself, "If money wasn't an issue here, what would I tell the client to do?"

Say, "Here's what I would do in your shoes." Lay out the prescription. Ask, "How does that sound to you?" before the money talk. Then suggest, "Let's try this for three months and meet here again to retest your progress. OK?"

When the client agrees, spell out their pricing options. If they say, "I can't afford it," ask how much of the plan they CAN afford. If their answer is $200, then say, "If my budget was $200 per month and I wanted to get as healthy as possible, I'd prioritize these two things." Meet again in three months and repeat the process.

Path 2: "I am satisfied with my progress." First, congratulate them. Then tell their story if you haven't already. Have your camera ready: "Fantastic! I'd love to brag you up a little. I think the entire world should know your story! Are you up for a short interview? Less than three minutes, I promise." Bring out your camera. Ask these three questions:

"What brought you to [our business] in the first place?"

"What are your new goals?"

"What's your favorite part of the [business] experience?"

Share the video on your social media channels later with a link back to your program. Remember your Affinity Marketing opportunity too: "Who has helped you MOST in this journey?" This is your opportunity to "thank up," to find an excuse to approach a new high-affinity client. You can take it to the next level with, "What can I do to thank that person?" Your offer should be a free intro session or a nutritional assessment or even a review of their current retirement savings plan, depending on what your business does. After you put the camera away, ask the client how to contact that person (get a phone number or email) and then get in touch right away.

The third step in bright spots is reinforcement. This section also has two parts:

· Internal reinforcement
· External reinforcement

The science of motivation is the science of success. That's why I study motivation more than I consider anything else. After more than two decades as a coach, I know the "homework" I assign is secondary to my client's desire to perform it. Here's what we know about motivation:

1. Success has to happen before you become motivated.
2. Success has to KEEP happening.
3. We don't always recognize progress when it happens. We're pretty hard on ourselves.

Internal reinforcement is the most important. Many businesses sell incremental improvements: a client loses one pound per week, or their portfolio gains ten dollars per month. Maybe the improvements in their marriage are hard to measure. Whatever you're selling, it's essential to have your clients recount the bright spots of your service. This will reinforce your value and give them a source of gratitude they probably don't have anywhere else in their lives.

Asking a client, "What went well for you this week?" creates an opportunity for them to reflect on their personal bright spots. Like us, most of our clients just go from fire to fire without hearing positive feedback. Cultivating gratitude and a sense of balance will help them improve their outlook on life. For example, in the Two-Brain Facebook group, we practice Bright Spots Fridays. Every week, nearly every entrepreneur recounts what went right for him or her. It helps them recognize their incremental gains and motivates them to keep working hard on their business. This is internal reinforcement.

External reinforcement comes from the business. A hairdresser who spends a few minutes scrolling through her clients' selfie posts and commenting, "You look great!" is a good move. But a hairdresser who finishes an appointment by saying, "You look amazing! Let's take a selfie in front of our logo!" is making a great move. She's praising the client, and sharing her success at the same moment the client feels most willing.

In a gym, taking a client's picture in front of a whiteboard that reads "I just did my first pull-up!" is great for everyone: the client, the coach, and the business. Pictures tell powerful stories. Making people feel famous is excellent external reinforcement. Where else can they go to feel that kind of recognition? Making people feel a way they can't anywhere else is the key to great retention (and great marketing).

These "personal best" pictures work in all industries. Dave Ramsey, the author of several personal budgeting books like *The Total Money Makeover*, uses this technique on his Instagram feed often. Beaming couples and families send him pictures of themselves celebrating "First financial baby steps" or "$250,000 in debt gone!" Couldn't it work for an attorney, a car salesman, or a dentist? Of course it can. Fewer things are more attractive to your clients than praise. Plant bright spots along their trail like breadcrumbs.

BUILDING A RETENTION STRATEGY

Most entrepreneurs know they need some kind of retention plan; however, most approach it with a bunch of random ideas. For a month, they might send birthday cards and then stop because they want to give out cool badges instead. The next month, they're handing out balloons and sponsoring a fun run. The stronger choice? Pick one strategy and stick to it. Here are a few proven winners.

Ask people, "What do you want now?" often. Ask them the first time you meet, and ask again on a recurring basis.

This goes much further than "What kind of haircut do you want this time?" It's really a review of their goals, and then a prescription based on what they want. My book *Help First* goes into this in great detail.

Your clients need to "win" with your service. That means constant reinforcement of success. Smart politicians list their wins for their local community in every press release. Video games make the first few levels easy on purpose. CrossFitters hit a new personal best almost every day. Martial arts schools award stripes and belts every time a client advances her skills. These little tokens—even those little "badges" that pop up on your phone—are meaningful and important, but entrepreneurs often ignore them.

Handwritten notes mean more than a text. Even if they're sent less often—maybe after every tenth haircut—they still carry far more retention value than a text after every appointment. The latter is still a good idea, though. Imagine getting a text that says, "Hey, how's the haircut today? Send me a pic of what you're doing!" the morning after having your hair done.

It's better if one person manages retention instead of spreading the job across a team. All of our companies have a "joy person" role. The joy person's job is to manage retention. As the farmer levels up, she'll be unable to maintain a one-on-one connection with every client, so she needs to find someone to fill that seat. Remember, if retention is everyone's responsibility, it's no one's responsibility.

Be quick to change. People seek novelty more than ever before. We're all tempted by choice. The key is to rise above the choice and be the "meta" connector. Tell clients when they should do a spin class (and offer it, if you can). Tell them when it's time to take a break, and schedule their return. Don't wait for them to book a cleaning or an eye measurement. Schedule them in for an exam just before summer, when they'll need sunglasses.

Encourage grouping outside your workplace. You don't have to sponsor a black-tie event, but if you encourage the patrons at your brewery to join a weekend bicycle event, you'll build that elusive "community" that everyone seeks.

Be among them. Go to their weddings and their funerals. Don't be a float in the parade. Be in the crowd. Exercise with them, or meet them for coffee. Firing a friend is tough.

Finally, teach your clients that the path to happiness is through gratitude. Celebrate bright spots in a private Facebook (or other online) group every week.

Whatever retention strategies you decide to employ, record a Standard Operating Procedure and execute on it diligently. As with anything in business, you're better off choosing one strategy and knocking it out of the park, as one of my clients, Judy, would learn in our work together.

CASE STUDY: THE DANCER

"I never have enough clients." Judy teaches dance. A former professional dancer, Judy came back to her hometown to open a dance studio to a lot of fanfare. She had been in music videos, knew musical celebrities, and was maybe the closest thing to Hollywood her city has ever seen. Her new dance studio attracted two types of clients:

- Kids who were dancing at other studios, but wanted to compete at dance
- Kids who had never taken a dance class before

And that suited Judy just fine. The kids who came from other studios could reach new levels of competitive dance with her teaching. She had the credentials and CV to prove it. And kids who had never taken a class had a great time. The school's first live recital was a huge hit.

But within two years, only the competitive dancers remained. And while they demanded triple the time, attention, and travel of the "fun" dancers, they paid only a tiny bit more. Judy said, "With all of the travel, costumes, hair, and makeup, the parents can't afford to pay more for their lessons." Still, she thought the school needed the competitive program to establish its credibility, and every September, when the competitive dancers paid their annual dues, she saw an influx of cash. "That part is nice," Judy added.

Unfortunately, five years in, the cash Judy makes in September seems to be running out earlier every year. To bridge the cash flow shortages, Judy runs an eight-week Learn to Dance! camp for kids, and sometimes for parents, though those are poorly attended. The first camps are heavily discounted to get kids in the door, and from there, Judy hopes they'll jump to the competitive program, which costs twelve times as much.

She doesn't make enough from the Learn to Dance! camps to pay a coach to run them, so Judy has been teaching those classes, choreographing the competitive kids, organizing their travel schedule, and setting up an annual local recital. She's tired and knows she needs to hire an assistant but just can't afford it.

"If I had ten more kids in the competitive program, I could hire a coach and focus on growing the business," she told me, but that will never happen. Judy would have no choice but to find her solution elsewhere. Here are the real problems that I saw:

- The competitive program makes artistic sense, but Judy is losing money and time on it.
- The jump from "fun eight-week intro" to "full-time commitment" is huge.
- Kids sign up to Learn to Dance! After eight weeks, they've learned to dance. Next, they'll learn how to do something else. The end of their client journey is built into their first experience.
- Until Judy takes herself out of delivery, she'll never have the time to learn how to grow her business.
- The "next ten clients" will always be a revolving door.

First, I asked Judy, "Why do people want to dance?" She seemed a little offended by my crazy question.

"Well, it's obvious" she began. "Because it's beautiful. It's an art that uses your whole body. You lose yourself in the music. Every little girl wants to be a ballerina."

"Everyone?" I asked.

"Well, most of them." She struggled to not roll her eyes at me.

"How many, as a percentage?" I asked. She actually sighed.

"I guess maybe not all of them. But I sure did! From the first time I saw a ballerina, it was all I could think about."

Now, you don't get to be a professional dancer without a lot of brains, so Judy saw where I was headed: the reason SHE wanted to become a dancer might not have been the reason everyone does. "I give up," she said. "You tell me. Why do people want to learn to dance?"

"I don't know," I said truthfully. "Let's ask them."

Judy's first piece of homework was to choose five parents and ask them, "Why did you sign your kid up for dance?" She wanted to start with the parents of the competitive kids. I asked her to wait and start with the recreational kids.

"I bet they sign up because it's cheap," she said. I disagreed but didn't tell her so. No parent is Googling, "Cheap dance lessons for kids" or asking their friends, "What's the cheapest activity you know in town?"

At our second meeting, Judy reported the results of her parent-teacher interviews.

"I guess I'm a bit surprised," she said. "Two of the parents said they danced as kids and put their daughters into dance because they loved it in their childhood. Three parents just said, 'They're so cute,' over and over. And one said she wanted her daughter to exercise. The child chose dance as an alternative to gymnastics or CrossFit." She looked a little guilty at that last one. Judy knows I still own the CrossFit gym beside the Two-Brain Business office.

I laughed. "Okay, next assignment," I said. "I want you to go back to those same parents. Bring them coffee. Thank them again for helping you out and ask them, 'What are your plans for when this session ends?'" Judy was avoiding eye contact, so I asked, "What's wrong?"

She said, "I appreciate what we're doing here, and I think I get it. But I need more clients NOW. How will this help me get more clients? My next session is only half full, and if I don't fill it, I won't even be able to pay an assistant to help. I won't have time to ask all these questions you want me to ask. I really, really just need more clients."

I got her to look at me, and then said, "No, you don't." I didn't want to get into an argument, so I quickly followed with "What if every one of these kids signed up for the next eight weeks?"

Judy said, "Well, the classes would actually be overfilled." She quickly added, "But I advertised that the eight-week discounted offer was only for new families. You want me to let them do it again?"

"Nah," I said. "In a couple of months, that whole thing will be gone. But I do want you to ask the parent what they plan to do next. And when they ask you what they should do, I want you to tell them honestly. Forget about the money part until later. Just be their coach."

Judy looked skeptical. I knew she was still scared and probably wanted to run out and boost a Facebook post or maybe even discount her eight-week Learn to Dance! program even further. But I knew she would ALSO talk to the parents because she was paying me for mentorship. And I was right.

Judy didn't wait for our next meeting, she texted me the next evening. "I just spoke to the first three parents," she wrote. "One just said, 'I'll have to ask my kid.' The other two asked me what they should do."

"What did you tell them?" I replied.

"I said that both of their kids were enjoying it, and they should sign up for the next eight weeks to keep up their momentum. After all, they already have their dance outfits, and most of the rookie aches and pains are gone. The hard part is behind them." Those two parents immediately agreed to sign up—at the regular rate—for more lessons.

"Did you feel like a saleswoman?" I asked, already knowing the answer.

"Not at all. I hate selling. I'm an artist!" she said.

I'm glad she couldn't see me smiling on the phone.

"So, do I give them the discount again?" she asked after a moment.

"No way," I said. "You don't need to. And you'd be unfaithful to your current clients if you did."

After experiencing a small win, Judy was more open to my advice, even though it was hard for her to get out of the discounting mindset. But after six years of mentoring entrepreneurs, I've learned to take things one small step at a time. Eventually, I would tell Judy to kill the competitive program. We would rebuild around the things parents wanted: fitness, fun, and a cute recital at the end. We would start paying Judy a little every week and then seek partnership with other dance schools in town instead of competing with them. For now, Judy is taking the core lessons of this experience—giving your best clients what they want, retaining the clients you have, and spending your time on those who'll say yes—and already gaining some traction.

There's one last piece I want to talk about: what should you do when your client (potential or current) only gives you a "maybe"?

GETTING CLIENTS OFF MAYBE

One of my first lessons in sales came from a consultant named Frank Foster. I was running the pro shop and ski school at a mountain resort. We had 130 coaches, a bunch of chalets, and a thousand pairs of rental skis. But we didn't have customers. Not enough, anyway.

My job was to approach ski clubs to sell weeklong getaway packages. I wasn't very good at it. So they brought in Frank. He told me:

> "The people who say yes are great. Obviously. The people who say no are also great because you can move straight to someone else. You get closer to a yes client when any client says no. You don't waste time. The ones you DON'T want are the 'maybe' clients. They cost you time. And they turn you into a salesman."

Frank's lesson was taught with a single scenario in mind: cold-calling. I still don't do it, but the "move them from maybe" lesson is essential for every client in your business.

Consider that a "sale" doesn't begin when a client walks through your door, and it doesn't end when they sign on the dotted line. The sale begins with a first impression. And it never ends. Before a client comes to the door, they should know your prices. They should know that you're an expert. And they should be presented with a solution to their unique problems. We teach all of that in our Affinity Marketing program.

When a client visits for the first time, you're going to spend time talking to them. You'll probably spend the same amount of time talking to them whether they sign up or not. Why not use your time talking mostly to those who'll say yes?

I own a couple of gyms. When the gyms were new, I didn't post our prices on our websites. We were the highest-priced gym in town, and I wanted the chance to explain our value to new clients. Out of every ten clients who came through the door, I would sign up four. The other six were always surprised that we charged many times more than the gym up the road. They said, "I have to think about it" or "I'll talk it over with my husband and call you next week." I invested my time into them on the slim hope that I could talk them into signing up. (Spoiler alert: you can't "talk someone into" painful exercise that costs half as much as their car payment.)

As we grew, I asked myself, "What if I only spent time with those four in ten who want to sign up?" Then I examined the common denominators in my yes clients and my no clients. Price was the dividing line. By placing the price of our service on our website, I could eliminate many of the maybes. I did. As predicted, our total number of consultations went down, but our yes rate went way up. And I spent the time saved on better things. Will some of those maybes come back? Maybe, when they're ready. But we won't chase them.

The fact is "the sale" never ends. On every visit to our gym, a client must be "sold" again: they must be encouraged to come back the next day. Habit helps. But we're a coaching gym: every client gets one-on-one attention every single day. And the community of exercisers in the gym is very high-touch. They do a lot of the "selling" for us. We have fun workouts and a positive atmosphere.

Sometimes, a client will slide from yes to maybe. When they do, we usually double down: we meet with them in person to ask how we can serve them better. We try a new exercise prescription instead. We change their focus. But if they're continually sliding back to maybe, we let them go to no. We focus on our yes clients instead. As you read earlier, pumping water and energy into a dead limb hurts the whole tree.

Bob Burg said, "Usually, you need to ask for the sale. But it needn't be anything fancy. Depending on your product or service it can be something as simple as, 'Would you like to get started?' Remember, if you've gone through the process correctly, including discovering their needs, wants, and desires, and connecting those with the benefits of your product or service, then at this point, you're simply asking them to do something that they've already told you they want to do."

THE FARMER'S ROLES

In the Farmer phase, the entrepreneur systematically replaces themselves in low-value roles and takes on higher-value roles. This can be explained using a ladder analogy. For example, if the farmer passes off cleaning ($15/hour, or $150 per week) and uses that time to generate more sales ($200 per week), then they have an ROI of $50 per week. They identify the next lowest-value role (programming?) and reinvest that time into a higher-value role (like marketing).

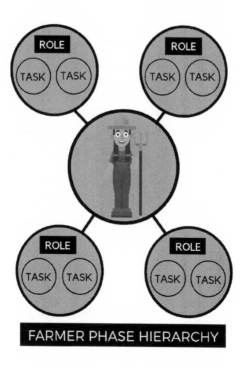

FARMER PHASE HIERARCHY

Moving from founder to farmer means "leveling up." You progress from buying yourself a job to owning a business. The Founder phase gave you the chance to OWN something, to build it any way you like, to kick away from bosses and fill your own cup. But this immense freedom can quickly turn into a trap. Starting a business is EASY. It's HARD to keep one going.

OPTIMIZE, AUTOMATE, OUTSOURCE

Ari Meisel is the cofounder of GetLeverage.com, an agency that matches specialists with entrepreneurs.

When we met in Manhattan, he underscored the importance of building repeatable systems in your business:

> If you have a process in your day, or your week, or your business that you do on a regular basis, those are processes that need to be documented, identified, and improved. Anything that can be made into a bulletproof process that can be followed by anybody isn't something that you should be doing because it's clearly not your unique ability.

He then repeated:

> By definition, if somebody else can do it, it's not a unique ability.

Most entrepreneurs are still reluctant to step outside themselves and view their business with an objective eye. Doing everything is comforting because it's familiar ground. It's tempting to think, "No one can make the donuts the way I do!" And entrepreneurs who don't really want to own a business can keep thinking that way. They're self-employed. They've bought themselves a job. But I suspect that's not why you're reading this book.

If the operation of the company and the growth of the company is always depending on you, then your business is not as strong as you think, and as scary as it might sound, stepping away from certain roles or functions is the best choice you can make for your company *and* your team.

Your employees making a living under your umbrella can be limited if the umbrella never rises. It's your duty to THEM—not just to yourself—to remove yourself from their work, give them the resources and vision to succeed, and then lift the umbrella higher for everyone.

WHO TO HIRE FIRST: THE ENERGY AUDIT

You first improve your EHR by moving low-value roles off your plate. These are the tasks that can easily be described in a checklist or "if-then" document. These are the roles that can be quickly filled by binary thinkers.

But replacements become more expensive as the roles become more complex. Specialists work for generalists, and as the tasks performed by your specialists rise in value, so does the cost of replacement.

Eventually, two roles of a comparable cost will emerge as the next to be removed from the farmer's plate. Or a farmer might hesitate to make a next-level hire because of the expense. If a software developer earns $80 per hour, and the farmer's EHR is under $50, they might wait to hire the specialist and muddle through themselves.

The Kingmaker equation is earned revenue over time. But there's really a third dimension: energy.

As the entrepreneur matures, their time becomes more valuable, and their energy becomes scarce. Decision fatigue, stress, and time all sap the entrepreneur's energy. Lack of focus, lack of fitness, and an increasing daily volume of distractions all draw from the energy bank. In the Tinker phase, I'll describe how to protect—and even grow—that energy reserve. But in the Farmer phase, the entrepreneur must be aware of their energy levels and protect them. For that reason alone, it's often essential to hire staff to replace you in work that drains you, leaving you free to pursue work that energizes you. How do you know which is which? Do an energy audit.

I learned this technique from my friend Trevor Mauch at Carrot (OnCarrot.com). Trevor runs a huge company that generates leads for real estate salespeople. In any given day, he can be pulled in a thousand different directions. But he's an influential leader because he spends his time working on tasks that provide him with energy and delegates everything else.

He told me, "We become entrepreneurs because we want four things: freedom, flexibility, finances, and impact.

"When you're doing work that zaps your energy, and also

when you're doing work in a business that has a boom and bust business model, you could be making great money, but during the year, you're stressed out. You lose your flexibility. You might have the finances, but you don't have the mental capacity or time to make the impact you want to make.

"This exercise literally 10Xed my income. It 10Xed my net profit well into seven figures. That's my net taxable income today. I'm not saying that to sound cool. I'm saying it because this process unlocked all of it."

Here's how to do it using the Roles and Tasks exercise results from the Founder section.

First, take a blank sheet of paper. Draw a vertical line down the middle.

At the top, in the left column, write "Gives Energy." In the right column, write "Drains Energy."

Now, take your list of roles from your Founder phase exercise. Copy the roles that give you energy into the "Gives" list. If they don't actively fire you up, copy them to the "Drains" list.

If you want to get really deep, do the exercise with tasks instead of roles (that list should contain hundreds of tasks instead of the dozen or so roles.) Any job that doesn't excite and energize you should be placed on the "Drains" list. The roles associated with that task should be delegated out first.

As you approach the hiring of managerial or specialty staff, first eliminate the roles with an EHR of less than $50. Then replace yourself according to the "Drains" list, retaining only the roles and tasks that fall on the "Gives" list.

This is a step toward the Tinker phase. Mauch publishes his Energy Audit for free at OnCarrot.com/energy.

YOUR FIRST "MANAGERIAL" HIRE

It should be obvious that the move from founder to farmer means moving from frontline delivery to management. And the move from farmer to tinker implies the introduction of a management layer in your hierarchy. But bridging that gap can be done in stages, and the first stage is to hire an administrator. You might call the administrator a general manager, or even a chief operations officer (COO).

The administrator role can be summed up like this: "Make sure the business operates at its current level." In even simpler terms: "Maintain what we currently have."

The administrator isn't in charge of growing the business. (That's still your job, for now.) Their job is to make sure your service is delivered smoothly and on time, that payments are appropriately processed, that clients are booked and serviced, and that staff gets paid.

The administrator might eventually grow into a managerial role in operations (or even become a director of operations themselves), but first, they must replace you in overseeing delivery. This role might include:

- Client communication
- Payment processing
- Payroll
- Financial reporting
- Staff evaluation
- Staff scheduling
- Building and equipment maintenance
- The intake and onboarding process

The role won't necessarily include:

- Marketing or outbound sales
- Delivering the service itself (i.e., cooking the donuts or coaching a fitness class)
- Cleaning (but would include the responsibility for having the cleaning done)

The primary difference between an administrator's role and any other role is the new gauntlet of responsibility. It's the administrator's responsibility to identify problems and fix them.

Other staff might report problems, but the administrator must solve problems.

The buck stops at the administrator's door. If the cleaner doesn't show up, it's the administrator's responsibility to find another cleaner or clean the office himself. The bottom line is that the administrator frees up the farmer's mental bandwidth by overseeing all of the day-to-day operations. They are the giver and evaluator of checklists.

WHAT SHOULD AN ADMINISTRATOR BE PAID?

Two factors go into deciding what each role should be paid:

1. The education required for the role
2. The burden of responsibility removed from the entrepreneur

An administrator will need to have college-level reading, speaking, and writing skills. But you, as the owner, will teach most of the job-specific duties. That means the base pay should be around 50 percent higher than the minimum wage.

Any additional responsibility should increase the base wage by around $5 per hour, depending on how many staff members need to be managed and the amount of revenue managed. Placing a $15-per-hour employee in charge of $2 million in revenues is probably asking for trouble.

This is probably the first role that warrants a salary because it's not time-specific but responsibility-specific. It goes without saying that some weeks will require flexibility in time. To that end, beware of the salary trap: work expands to fill the space you give it. An administrator hired to "work forty hours" will always be busy but accomplish less than an administrator hired to "complete these forty tasks." Time-creep happens to many entrepreneurs (you can be very busy without actually accomplishing anything of value), and it happens even more often to employees because our education system has taught them that attendance is more important than results.

THE FARMER'S ROLE PROGRESSION

To move up to Tinker phase, you need at least one person in a position of responsibility for the others. That's usually the "administrator" role, even if it's part-time. (Fifteen hours per week will work in most owner-operator businesses.)

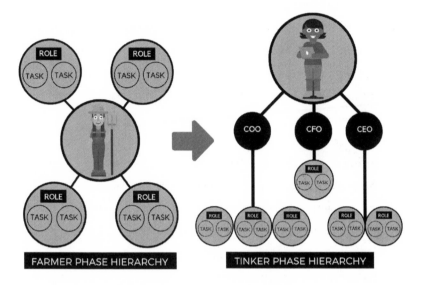

FARMER PHASE HIERARCHY

TINKER PHASE HIERARCHY

CORE CONCEPT: GET OUT OF YOUR OWN WAY

It's 5 a.m. on Monday morning, and you've decided this is going to be a productive day—maybe even an all-caps PRODUCTIVE DAY.

You're whipping the ghee into your coffee, going through the mental checklist of all the business development tasks you're going to work on today once you get to the gym and get things going. You've got a cool idea for a member contest and need to sort out the details and get it announced on your website, newsletter, and blasted on social media. There's also the issue of your lease coming up for renewal in a year, and you're considering expanding by moving to a new space.

You arrive at the gym as your trusted 6 a.m. coach is writing the workout on the whiteboard and looking after the early birds doing their mobility work. You sit down in your office and listen to the voicemail, making a note to get back to the two potential new clients and the juice supplier who needs your credit card for this month's order. You open the gym's "info@" email account and start sorting through the spam and answering the customer information questions. Soon a client pokes their head in to let you know there's a leaky tap in the men's locker room. After dealing with that, you notice that the towel bin is full again and that the soap needs refilling. You're right there, so you take care of it. On the way back to the office, a client pulls you aside to ask if they can upgrade their membership, so you happily bring them into the office to process their payment.

It's time for your morning meeting with your two managers, and it takes a little longer than you'd like explaining to them what next month's programming is going to entail. While the meeting was going on, your Facebook page blew up with alerts, so you grab the assistant manager who helps with social media and you describe how to moderate a discussion among members about shaving reps that is getting a little too heated for your liking.

You look up at the clock. It's almost noon, and you haven't even started on that contest, never mind called the landlord about the lease.

Sound familiar?

If it does, you're not alone. Research suggests only 30 percent of managers believe they are good at delegation, which is a critical obstacle blocking your path to real leadership and taking your business to the next level.

Delegating is more than just giving tasks to your staff. It's empowering them to make decisions and execute the business plan. Not only does this free you as an owner to devote your energy to high-level directing that will grow your business, but it also develops leadership skills in your people and strengthens the whole team.

THE EIGHT LEVELS OF DELEGATION

1. **"Do it like this."** Instructing your staff this way makes sure it's "done right," which satisfies the perfectionist in you but leaves no freedom for your delegate to make decisions themselves.
2. **"Look into this and tell me the situation. I'll decide."** Your staff is empowered to give you analysis but not recommend action. You've still kept the responsibility of evaluating the options and making the decision.

3. **"Look into this and tell me the situation. We'll decide together."** It's a subtle difference, but here you're enabling the decision-making process to be shared, which promotes development in your staff.

4. **"Tell me the situation and what help you need from me in assessing and handling it, after which we'll decide."** Here, your staff has the extra responsibility to ask themselves questions you would have posed at the previous level of delegation, combined with shared decision-making.

5. **"Give me your analysis of the situation and the pros and cons of your recommendation. I'll let you know whether you can go ahead."** You're acting as a check on your staff's discretion but show trust in their ability to make sound decisions and implement solutions. Be careful that your approval doesn't delay the process, which can create frustration.

6. **"Make your decision and inform me of it, then go ahead unless I say not to."** By default, you're in agreement with your staff member, which empowers them even further. It also removes barriers to action if they know that they can act unless they hear otherwise by a specific deadline.

7. **"Decide and implement the solution, and then let me know what happened."** You save even more time with this level of responsibility while building in follow-up and feedback. This coaching method builds

confidence and develops big-picture decision-making skills that align with your business values.

8. **"Decide and take action. It's all you!"** This level moves entirely into the realm of mentorship. You provide feedback on a more periodic basis and grant strategic responsibility. Your staff defines projects, tasks, implementation, and analysis, making the necessary decisions in their area of responsibility. This highest level of delegation is appropriate for training a successor, co-owner, or someone preparing to strike out on their own and build their own gym!

Your challenge is to push yourself to progress from a do-everything or a level-1 delegator to levels 5 and beyond. You've hired great people who you want to be challenged and grow, just like your clients challenge themselves in your gym. It's time to build their strengths, get out of your own way, and free yourself to lead your business into the future you envision.

THE FARMER'S MENTOR

Founders need business coaching, but the TYPE of coaching they need will differ. Some will require systems to follow (closer to a franchise model). Others will take ideas from other businesses and apply them (peer modeling). And still others will see opportunities and rise to meet them.

Other times, it might mean presenting a picture of the industry and saying, "Here's what's working in San Diego, and how it can be modified to fit your law practice in Massachusetts." And for many, it means, "There's a massive opportunity to add a tutoring service," or, "It's time to open another bakery." When a client asks, "What's next?" I get very excited. But not every owner will want a second location or another business, and in those cases, a mentor can best help by presenting the best systems.

Mentorship in the Farmer phase focuses on accountability, resilience, and growth. A good mentor in the Founder phase keeps the founder focused on building core services and creating business processes. At Two-Brain Business, we plan our mentorship in annual cycles and start the year by asking five questions:

- What do you want to earn this year?
- What do you want to learn this year?
- Where do you want to travel this year?
- What do you need to upgrade this year?
- Who will you serve this year?

Then we set a Kingmaker goal for time spent in the business. Dividing that goal into their earnings goal will create a target for Effective Hourly Rate. Then we calculate their profit margin and determine how much revenue they'll need for the year. We break that goal down by month and then by revenue stream. That will give us a clear picture of where they're headed, and their mentor can begin to map their process.

Since most entrepreneurs answer "more!" to the first question, that map usually includes a plan to increase profit margin, diversify revenue streams, and add top-line revenue through marketing. Every month, the farmer and mentor talk over live video and walk through their progress. Then they set a course for the next month. This accountability component is a large part of our own corporate values at Two-Brain Business.

Another of our values is peer support. We place entrepreneurs in private groups of supportive peers in their own phase. We all know that doubts don't usually spring up during a regularly scheduled appointment time. They creep up on us at 3 a.m., when we're alone with our thoughts. Using online groups, we can provide round-the-clock support, feedback, and celebration to the Two-Brain Business family.

Eventually, success in business ownership means more than being a good baker or trainer. Ownership is a different skillset entirely.

It took Elliott Jaques nearly fifty years to develop his theories around stratification of job tasks. I'll try to sum it up in five minutes.

Disclaimer: this is not a commentary on anyone's intelligence, potential, or raw brainpower. To the contrary, the purpose here is to identify friction and cognitive dissonance. If you're working at things you like, you'll be happy and achieve your "perfect day." And that's always the point. Different owners find joy at different levels, according to Jaques.

Level 1—Analog: "I do THIS and THIS, and then I do THIS." Step by step. No further processing required. Not usually a great level for owners, but some staff will fit here. In our businesses, we've been lucky enough to hire Harry to do the cleaning. Harry loves a useful checklist. "First, I sweep the 'big room.' Then I sweep the hallways. Then I mop the big room. Then I mop the hallways." Harry LOVES to clean. He's passionate about it. He's loyal to a certain brand of toilet bowl cleaner. He doesn't question his wage or dread coming to work. He's excited to be part of our team and collect a check on Friday.

Level 2—Binary: "I do this. If this happens, THEN I do this." The algebra of the task expands, but the paths are still linear. Decisions are automatic (predetermined in your staff handbook) but enforced by the level-2 worker. This may be a shift supervisor or a manager, and some business owners can be successful with this type of thinking: phone scripts, marketing "funnels" and other prewritten plans. "Just tell me what exactly to say and do."

Level 3—Algebraic: This is where most good business owners sit. They see the long tail. They recognize the long-term plan that dictates the short-term work. They're good at business (and don't refer to their job as "the business side" of their operation because they know there's no such thing). They do some forecasting and planning. At this level, most of the delivery portion of their business is managed or automated. This is where many owners are most happy. The business is sustainable, they don't have to show up all the time, and they're making a comfortable living.

Up to this point, the system has been mostly mathematical. The transition from level 3 to level 4, however, is like the transition from ice to water. The farmer is entirely different from the founder.

Level 4—Entrepreneurial: A viewer of "the big picture." An understanding of HOW and WHY. Like level 1, the entrepreneur finds joy in working. Like level 2, the entrepreneur likes applying the advice of others. Like level 3, the entrepreneur finds satisfaction from building and self-reliance. But unlike the others, the entrepreneur enjoys building custom solutions to new problems. The entrepreneur usually enjoys a bit of risk. And the entrepreneur is an adventurer.

For example: a client is dissatisfied and wants their money back.

Level 1 says: "Not my job. Ask my supervisor."

Level 2 says: "Our policy says no refunds."

Level 3 says: "If I give this person their money back, it sets a precedent that may hurt ALL the staff in the next few years. We want to grow out AND up, and we need a solid foundation and rules from which levels 2 and 3 can draw so they don't have to stress about this stuff."

Level 4 says: "WHY do they want their money back? What service should we really be providing to this client?"

Jaques's levels actually go up to 12, but for our discussion, let's end there. Now, the most critical part: guiding owners to joy, and that starts with the right role. Here are some potential approaches to mentorship:

- The owner who loves coaching so much that he decides to open his own gym. He's miserable for the next three years because he hates bookkeeping and scheduling and lawyers and cash flow and overhead. Worst of all, he coaches less than ever because he doesn't have time. For him, systems to automate the business will mean more time coaching.

- The owner who's great at delivering a high-quality experience every day. He loves accounting, but his clients won't accept anyone else's hands in their books. This requires a custom process involving time and trust. Mentoring is necessary to move from one system to the next.

- The owner who's chasing a headcount instead of a "perfect day." She believes she "just needs more clients." For this owner, one-on-one mentoring is a must because their paradigm needs to change. And change is impossible without a guide.

- The owner whose business is ticking along, providing a significant income and a career for others. Now they see opportunities but don't know which to pursue, or in what order, or how to free themselves from the business, or how to retire. These folks need an "eye in the sky" to keep them moving forward and an appropriate level of challenge. Being an entrepreneur doesn't mean owning more than one business. It just means seeking opportunities and finding new ways to win.

Placing an owner in a role where they're most happy is

the job of a real mentor. I'm most satisfied when a client takes a weekend off for the first time or sends me texts celebrating a lifestyle goal. Numbers are great (they make the world go 'round), but they're not the endgame. Our endgame is joy.

THE FARMER'S CHALLENGES

Before industrialization, the population of the Western world was scattered into small pockets of self-sufficiency. Most homes had at least one food source on hand (a family chicken or goat or a fruit tree). Farmers with two food sources were more resilient and wealthy, so they traded their surplus or bought the property of others.

After World War I, many farmers were pulled to cities to make a better life. Instead of the subsistence-level income they earned on the farm, they could own a car and washing machine. So they sold the farm to a neighbor and got a job instead. But the neighbor also became wealthier. As he acquired more land, his food sources multiplied. His surplus crops grew. And if his surplus rose faster than another neighbor, he could purchase their property too.

As farmers moved into the vast machinery of the city, more crops were needed to feed them. And industrialization loves specialization. It's easier to buy a lot of wheat from one farmer than a little bit of grain from a dozen. So farmers specialized their crops and eventually industrialized their farms. Today, large conglomerates own most of the farmland in the Western hemisphere. Small farmers can't produce meat or wheat at scale, so they charge more for it. Wheat is a commodity, which means the bread companies buy it at the lowest price they can. Industrial farms can sell it cheaply because they grow so much.

An entrepreneur in the Farmer phase has to compete. Many will compete with large "factory" businesses. They'll never grow enough wheat to compete on price, so they have to compete on quality and service instead. But this is a significant advantage. The challenges of the Farmer phase are to identify the clients who want high quality, tailor the offering to match those people, and price the service at a level that will support the farm.

Farmers will have to deliver their product at a high level of consistency because working with high-value clients means never delivering a single low-value donut. Buyers who are seeking "average" will also seek the lowest price, and those who seek the best will want the best every time, not "usually better." And all the while, competition will try to eliminate the farmer.

The challenges you'll face at this stage can be big—even

terrifying—and it's going to take more than work to surmount them.

THE BUSY BEAVER

One of our cultural symbols for hard work is the beaver. You'll see beavers in cartoons (often wearing a hard hat), children's fables about hard work and resilience, and even on the back of the Canadian nickel. It's our natural animal. It's also a rodent. And a nuisance to any human who owns the land on which a beaver builds their dam.

For those who don't know, a beaver survives by building a dam across a stream and flooding the local area. He chews down whole trees with his big front teeth, pulls the trees through the water, and cements them into the dam with mud and grass. As the barrier grows, the water level rises. Then he builds a lodge—a massive mound of mud—and raises his family. He swims underwater and carries food back to the lodge, then spends the rest of his time growing his dam.

He'll never stop growing his dam. His beaver pond will gradually consume more and more of the land around it, and more beavers will join him as the pond increases.

I have a beaver on my property now. Like a farmer, he works hard to grow his dam and, thereby, his family. And like the industrialist, I work hard to stop him because I don't want his pond in my basement.

For a few weeks, I watched him grow his pond. It was exciting to see his dam grow, and I romantically compared him to a hardworking entrepreneur. Ducks and geese began to quack around in the water, and the singing frogs at night were beautiful in the spring.

But then he flooded out my bridge. And the water levels rose to threaten an old barn. He cut off most of my property from the house. Eventually, I decided he had to move on.

So I pulled down part of his dam—maybe a three-foot section out of a hundred-foot span. I watched the water run out at an enormous rate and marveled at his creation again. Then I went to bed, confident the beaver would be gone by morning. But by morning, the dam was fixed. It was fixed and bigger.

So I ripped open my original hole and created a second one. Water coursed downstream. The beaver—ordinarily nocturnal—swam out to inspect the damage. I threw a stick near him to scare him, and he swam away.

Three hours later, both holes were fixed, and the water was rising.

Now he had my full attention. I found a local trapper and hired him, thinking, "I'll never take the dam down fast enough. I have to eliminate the beaver." I'd had enough. Spending hours ripping down beaver dams was tearing me away from my real work as a business mentor and even interrupting my travel schedule.

When the trapper arrived at my door, he asked, "How many beavers do you want me to trap?"

I said, "Keep going until they take the beaver off our money." In other words, I wanted all of them GONE. Within three days, the trapper had removed six beavers from our property. I punched a third hole in the dam to let it drain, then boarded a flight for New Jersey, happy in the knowledge that my backyard would be dry when I returned.

It wasn't.

Within forty-eight hours, the dam was repaired and growing.

Now, I have far more resources than the beaver. I can rent tractors and hire trappers. I can outlast him and pull holes in his dam faster than he can fix them. A beaver is the stereotypical picture of hard work, but that's his only asset. I'm smarter. And I have a tractor.

After a few weeks, the beaver was gone. He couldn't out-work my resources. Beavers are admirable, but they're rodents. They can't outthink a human. The trapper caught the beaver and moved him back into the hills.

Many entrepreneurs in the Farmer phase have convinced themselves that hard work is the straight and true path to success. It's not. The real way to success is resilience and growth.

The trapper used a beaver trap made of black metal and powerful springs. But what really caught the beaver was its habit of returning to the same work every single day and hoping for a different result. When we moved the 1,032nd stick on the dam, he'd replace that same stick. His predictability ultimately defeated him.

If the beaver were capable of cultivating crops under-water and surviving in a smaller pond, he'd still be here. Or if he could climb trees instead of cutting them down, he'd still be here. If he could have recruited more beavers and worked faster or differentiated his work or partnered with owls to deliver food back to his lodge, he'd still be here. But he's not. Doing the same thing over and over is a recipe for burnout and failure.

As an entrepreneur transitions from founder to farmer, she will encounter opposition from established businesses. These existing companies usually pay no mind to the hobbyist or part-timer, but as the new enterprise grows, it will attract their attention. And they won't be friendly. Corporations and veteran owners have larger budgets. They have loyal clients and market awareness. But they also have sunk costs, a rigid mindset, and they're slow to change. The larger the company, the more invested they are in the status quo. As the legendary Mel Siff once told me, "As soon as you plant your flag, people will start shooting."

The tactics shared in this section will help the farmer grow a business from a startup to a meaningful company. Creating systems and processes are necessary to keep the entrepreneur nimble. But the farmer's significant advantage is still her energy and passion. She can choose to use that energy on low-value roles (delivering the donuts herself) or high-value roles (growing the customer base, expanding her service, and diversifying). If she chooses the former, she loses like the beaver. But if she leaves good tracks for her staff to follow, builds a resilient infrastructure, and focuses on the battles she can WIN, she will.

Success in the Farmer stage doesn't mean having the largest gross revenue. It doesn't mean having the most clients. Neither of those metrics is meaningful, and they're not a reasonable goal—yet.

Success in the Farmer stage means creating a reliable income for an entrepreneur and his staff, creating a long-term cash flow asset, working toward a 33 percent profit margin (or better), and changing lives in the process.

THE MULE TRAP

"This is all I know. This is all I have. And I'll die in this gym if I have to." I had that mantra stuck to my desk for a couple of years. It's a song lyric. And it's all you need to know about my mindset as a young entrepreneur.

"I will lead this horse to water and hold its head under until it drinks." I actually wrote that on a blog post in 2010. I still believed in martyrdom then. I still believed that the hustle was the answer. Gary Vaynerchuk wasn't a household name then. No gym owners were talking about "the grind." But every morning at 5 a.m., before the lights at the gym even warmed up, I'd press my cheek against the front window and look down the street to make sure my gym was open before the others on the block.

I wanted to believe that the hardest worker would win. I told myself that lie because I know I can outwork anyone. If putting your head down and trudging forward—in sickness and in health, for better or for worse—made a business successful, then I was a born winner.

If the volume of work was the answer, I had a huge advantage: I'd been trained for work since birth. Trudging through the snow to a frozen stream in the dark, chopping a hole through the ice with an ax, hauling pails uphill to meet thirsty animals that wanted to butt me aside? Yeah, I did that. At age eight. I've been on sinking boats. I've followed the blood trail of a wounded bear without a rifle. I've passed out in hayfields from heatstroke and then finished the day. I worked on a logging crew in college. I have frostbite in both ears and most of my toes to remind me of my first job as a rink caretaker.

Those are all cool stories. And none of them matter a bit.

I was a mule. I was never late. I drove my truck past "Road Closed" barricades to get to work and had to be rescued by snowmobile. I once hit one hundred days without a day off from the gym. None of that made me profitable. I missed my kids for days at a time. I left home before they woke up and got home after they were in bed. I told myself, "I'm willing to do ANYTHING for them. And if they don't see my sacrifice, that's one more burden I'm willing to bear." Martyrdom is a romantic delusion. Here's what broke the spell.

A friend's business failed. He said, "I take pride in knowing that I did everything I could. It wasn't my fault the business went under." He had the luxury of blaming someone else. I didn't. And I asked myself, "Am I okay with this business dying, as long as it's not MY fault?" That would have proven my martyrdom, wouldn't it? Wasn't I already fantasizing about a buyout or a cooperative takeover that would have absolved me from the responsibility of failure?

When I zoomed out and looked at the situation objectively, I saw myself working hard toward an inevitable end. This business was going to fail. My kids were going to go without. And it didn't matter if it was my fault. It was my responsibility. Then I realized the greatest thing in my way was my ego. I WANTED to believe that hard work wins because that's my strength. I wanted to believe that starting my day at four gave me an advantage over someone who started at five because I was good at the 4 a.m. start. I did NOT want to ask for help. Hell no.

The real "park bench moment" came for me when I realized that I couldn't possibly work any harder and that success wasn't any closer. I literally asked, "What if I did the opposite of everything I'm currently doing?" I hired a mentor. I took his advice. I actually paid for it, which was anathema to me. I did what he said to do, even if it seemed counterintuitive.

The hardest part was when my mentor said, "Take a day off." I think my response was, "Okay. What should I do on my day off?" (This is like saying, "I'll do a few reps while I'm resting between rounds of exercise.") I don't take time off well. That's a huge weakness of mine. So is stubbornness. But my greatest weakness is my willingness just to work MORE, work HARDER, instead of stopping to ask, "What am I doing?" I still fall into the mule trap. I try to do everything. I wake up at 1 a.m. with an idea to help gym owners and go sit on the couch with my laptop. The lure of work is strong, but it often pulls me away from doing the RIGHT things. It's not a virtue; it's a trap.

When you farm for a living, the ability to bow your head and pull the plow is an asset. I come from generations of people like that. But when you open a business, you need to lift your eyes to the horizon. Thank you to my mentors for showing me the light.

FREE RANGE

Even when we know what we SHOULD do, we often need a rule—or a fence—to guide our actions and remove the burden of choice. Dr. Temple Grandin is a professor of animal science at Colorado State University. She's the author of several books, including *The Way I See It* and *Thinking in Pictures*. She's been featured on NPR, BBC, *Larry King Live*, *60 Minutes*, and virtually every news show you've ever seen. And she has autism.

Grandin is an expert in animal behavior because her autistic brain sees in pictures. When she looks at cows going to the slaughter, she can picture what they see and help make their voyage simpler. Instead of using whips and electric barbs to keep the cattle going, Grandin understands that the poor animal just doesn't know what to do and shows the farmer how to place their fences and gates to keep the cow moving ahead.

We have a huge neocortex, and the ability to imagine every possible scenario and outcome has kept our species alive for millennia. But in the modern age, it burdens us with anxiety and stress: we see problems where there really aren't any and put too much emphasis on what COULD happen instead of what's likely to happen. We overthink, we prethink, and we stress for no reason.

Often, removing the burden of choice is liberating. Mike Michalowicz told me, "The business itself does not need to change. The mind of the entrepreneur, the business owner running their business, is changed, and when you take your profit first, it forces that mind to kick into high gear and find innovative ways to get things done." Comparing the pros and cons of many options is exhausting because your brain has to switch between images and opportunities quickly. For example, let's imagine you're choosing which shirt to wear to work.

The yellow one is clean but only goes with the blue suit, which is not clean. But maybe it could work with the green suit.

The blue one would go with the green suit but not the black shoes.

The brown one would go well without a coat, but it's too warm outside for a thick shirt.

And as you rotate between choices, your brain reloads the data on each option. Your internal hard drive spins. And you get tired.

Steve Jobs wore the same turtleneck and jeans every day because he wanted to avoid decision fatigue. He ate the same breakfast and laced up the same shoes every day. Then, when he had a significant decision to make, he wasn't doing it with a tired brain: he was saving his brainpower for big decisions. He imposed the constraints of dress and food on himself. He made them a rule. He removed the burden of choice.

A big philosophical paradox is Buridan's ass. Imagine a donkey is placed between a pile of hay and a trough of water. The donkey is equally hungry and thirsty. Since the donkey will choose whichever is closer, and they're equidistant, he'll be unable to pick and will die of hunger and thirst.

As adults, we usually understand that any decision is better than none, and move toward either the food or the water. But we still agonize over the decision. The anticipation is often worse than the act. And delay, in business, can be fatal.

As entrepreneurs, we're rarely required to choose between a great opportunity and a poor one. More often, we're asked to choose between two equal opportunities: Do we invest in the new website company or sell more tickets for our event? The burden of choice is unusually heavy when both options are potentially good.

And that's why we need fences. We need laws to tell us when to pay our staff because it would be tempting to wait another week. We need autodeductions in our bank accounts because there are a thousand better things to do with our money than to pay the bank more interest or fees. I need a fitness coach to tell me exactly what to do, how many times, and how fast. I don't have time to sift through magazines and compare workout options. Some of the fences you need to consider in your business include:

When you'll get paid. This must be nonnegotiable. Follow the Profit First framework if you need external control: open separate bank accounts and write yourself checks in advance, then deposit them months ahead of time.

Which ideas you'll pursue this year. In his excellent book *Anything You Want*, Derek Sivers makes the point that you can do anything, but you can't do everything at once. My own business mentor has me choose three projects each year and focus on those. Every other option gets put on my calendar for next year. When January hits, we evaluate the possible projects that are waiting and then make a decision to act on three. Many times, some of the tempting options lose their luster in a few months.

Who you'll talk with on a daily basis. You really have the mental bandwidth to remember five conversations. If you have twelve staff reporting to you, you'll get buried in their ideas and complaints. Limiting your interactions helps your staff get their questions answered more efficiently and enables you to take action on growing your business.

While we're at it, here are some fences you'll want in your personal life:

1. Brush your teeth at the same time every day
2. Pay yourself enough to feed your kids
3. Exercise with a coach
4. Schedule vacations and family time

After all, your business exists to serve YOU. Delayed gratification is part of growing a business, but it's a sticky trap.

It's all too easy to put off the important goals and just keep showing up.

There's one more fence I want to talk about before we move on to the next challenge, one I call "Give it twenty-four hours," and I'm going to introduce it with a little help from a proverb I heard a few years ago.

Once upon a time, there was an old farmer who had worked his crops for many years. One day his horse ran away. Upon hearing the news, his neighbors came to visit. "Such bad luck," they said sympathetically, "you must be so sad."

"We'll see," the farmer replied.

The next morning the horse returned, bringing with it two other wild horses.

"How wonderful," the neighbors exclaimed! "Not only did your horse return, but you received two more. What great fortune you have!"

"We'll see," answered the farmer.

The following day, his son tried to ride one of the untamed horses, was thrown, and broke his leg. The neighbors again came to offer their sympathy for his misfortune.

"Now your son cannot help you with your farming," they said. "What terrible luck you have!"

"We'll see," replied the old farmer.

The following week, military officials came to the village to conscript young men into the army. Seeing that the son's leg was broken, they passed him by. The neighbors congratulated the farmer on how well things had turned out. "Such great news. You must be so happy!"

The man smiled to himself and said once again, "We'll see."

The lesson here is to stop reacting to things you can't control. Easier said than done, I know. When I read a negative comment about me on Facebook, my first reaction is to jump all over the person who posted it. I'm impulsively drawn to online battles. I can barely resist them. But they NEVER help me. I never feel better after engaging. I'm sure no one does. That's why I built a fence. My rule is to wait twenty-four hours before responding to an aggravating comment on social media. After twenty-four hours, I ask myself, "Can I just delete the comment?" Then I think, "Can I wait another twenty-four hours?"

Sometimes, if one seems especially egregious, I'll read it out loud to my wife. We usually laugh about it. Something about hearing the comment out loud puts it in the right context.

Then I'll ask myself, "Will I even remember this in a year?"

Finally, I'll procrastinate by distracting myself from the distraction.

By that point, the emergency has usually passed. And I'm usually the better for having ignored it.

We all tend to imagine the worst-case scenario: that one little setback will bankrupt our business. Our insecurities are magnified tenfold before we gain the experience to see the long view. For example, a consulting company in the gym industry once wrote a "rebuttal" to one of our blog posts. Their motives were clear only to us: they wanted to tiptoe into our spotlight. So they tagged us on Facebook, put videos on Instagram, and tried to link themselves to our brand in any way they could. I was very tempted to react. It would have been easy. Their blog post was poorly written and failed to make any counterpoint. It was a desperate cry for attention. But I waited.

The next morning, my email list had gained eighty new readers.

A month later, it had grown by over six hundred—mostly

clients of our critic, who were curious about what ELSE we were saying. Many of those clients upgraded to our service.

In another example, a local television personality was filming a series at the Workshop (our center for entrepreneurship). She raved about the space and staff on her Facebook page. One of her fans commented that our coworking space was too expensive and that our mentors weren't volunteers giving free opinions.

The show host was worried that such a "negative comment" would harm our business. But I knew better. Within twenty-four hours, we had two new coworking clients who were eager to avoid the noise and chaos of lower-priced alternatives.

It's usually easier to take SOME action than to take none. But reacting isn't the same as responding. A careful, measured response—even if the reaction is to do nothing—is easier for mature founders. But it's a skill that must be practiced and can be practiced even by new entrepreneurs.

Will that poor review really hurt your business?

Will that Facebook video really turn people away from your brand?

Will that staff departure really take all your clients and bankrupt you?

We'll see.

THE HARD PART: $2 MILLION TO $5 MILLION

Adolescence is pretty rough. You talk like a kid. You still like kids' stuff. But you're also taking on more responsibility. You're learning fast. And suddenly: feelings, growing pains, acne.

Many successful entrepreneurs point to their "adolescent" period as the toughest. Usually found between $2 million and $5 million in gross revenue, this period is often called "the valley of death." Here's why:

- The customer base is growing, and the staff is struggling to keep up
- Systems built for 100 clients don't scale to 1,000 clients
- The owner moves from frontline to back-office and doesn't have the new leadership skills required
- Higher-value roles are very expensive and feel like big bets
- No one knows for sure if growth will continue
- The staff that got them to $2 million probably won't be the same staff they'll have at $5 million

In short, a company that reaches $2 million in gross revenue probably won't be the same company that reaches $5 million in gross revenue. Its people will change, its customers might change, and its services will definitely change. That means a lot of unpredictability, a few scars, and acne. It also means the death of many companies. Not long ago, adolescent males were sent into the wild to "prove" they were men. Many failed and didn't return to camp. And this happens with companies too. Founders see massive growth and expect it to continue indefinitely, or they try to compete with huge companies, or they sell. Sometimes, the founder isn't the right CEO anymore.

The path between $2 million and $5 million is a long trudge up a steep slope. It means carrying the burden of "the way we've always done things" and sunk costs, staff relationships, and client aversion to change. It also means the willingness to admit that what got you *here* won't get you *there*. As difficult as that idea might be, I want you to start wrapping your head around it now.

Just as humankind moved from a "kill-and-eat-it" to an agrarian to an industrial economy, your business will grow from "get money wherever you can" to "plant and harvest" to automation. Many of those methods were explained in the Founder section of this book. But knowing the methods is only half the solution. Execution is the other half. Action—in farming and in business—is everything. Consistent, imperfect action grows crops, breeds calves, and builds businesses.

If consistent execution is the key to a business's growth, what's required for consistent execution? The FOUNDER'S growth. The skills that made you a great founder aren't the same skills required to make you a great entrepreneur. Sorry. In the next part of the book, we'll work on the limiting factor behind most business stagnation: its owner.

ARE YOU READY TO BE A TINKER?

Have you hired an "administrator" to oversee the client journey?

Have you begun managing staff instead of performing frontline duties?

Have you done an energy audit?

Have you launched at least one opportunity for intrapreneurship?

Have you hired at least one replacement for yourself in your primary service?

Have you done the "apples" and "weeds" client exercise?

Have you fired one "weed" client?

Have you started hosting regular staff meetings?

Have you begun to extend your marketing to people you don't yet know?

Have you started a retention strategy and taught it to your staff?

Have you budgeted for a staff development program?

Have you begun evaluating your staff quarterly?

Have you reached 33 percent gross profit margin?

Have you started tracking your enhanced metrics: leads, conversion rate, and revenue streams?

Have you started doing any paid lead generation?

Have you started attending a coached fitness program?

PART THREE

——

TINKER

"*For this reason, they must believe in the cause for which they are fighting. They must believe in the plan they are asked to execute, and most important, they must believe in and trust the leader they are asked to follow.*"

—JOCKO WILLINK, *EXTREME OWNERSHIP: HOW U.S. NAVY SEALS LEAD AND WIN*

The crops are growing. The storms are weathered. Each changing season sees a larger farm running smoothly without the farmer's steady hand on the tiller. So why is he so stressed out? Isn't this the life of leisure promised by entrepreneurship in the first place?

The revelation that "What got me here might not get me there" applies to people as well as to money, processes, and tactics. And eventually, every successful founder will need to ask himself: "What if I'm not the one to take this business to the next level?" The best founders aren't always the best CEOs. In a one-person company, that could mean the business fails to reach its peak potential, but when staff members are on the line, you have to put the best CEO at the top of the pyramid. And that means you must *find* the best leader or *become* the best leader.

As a tinker, you have four priorities.

The first is what is called **asset priority**. You want to make sure your business is a real cash flow asset, meaning it runs itself but still pays you. The biggest asset you have is your time, and you need it freed up to work on the most critical tasks.

The second priority is **leverage**. Leverage is the way you use your time best. Is it easier to start a brand-new business, or would it be easier to build on the niche you already know and serve them in a new way? Which would be the best use of your skills, tools, audience, and clients?

The third priority is what I call **low-hanging fruit**: asking yourself, "What is the easiest new thing to do?" This might be adding a dietician practice to your gym or improving your intake system.

The fourth and final priority is asking, **"What do my**

best clients want?" "How else can I serve them?" You should care enough about your clients that you are willing to solve other problems for them.

The Founder and Farmer sections of this book focused on building the business. Tinker focuses on building the entrepreneur. It holds the best stories, lessons, and tactics for building leadership in you. It will touch on behavior, psychology, and mental and physical training because all are necessary to lead your tribe into the larger frontier. These skills and strengths (which I call "fitnesses") aren't inherent; they're trained. There are no born leaders, just good leaders and bad. And the good leaders have many dents.

At this level, success isn't determined by how much work you do IN your business. It's not determined by how much work you do ON your business either. Your success will be defined by the work you do on yourself.

Get ready for the hardest stage of all.

THE TINKER'S KEYWORD: ABDICATION

It's time for you to move out of the daily operations of your first business to pursue more significant opportunities. It may mean duplication: opening a second location, licensing your model to others, or scaling up to a larger niche. It could be diversification: purchasing buildings or investing in other businesses to develop multiple cash flow assets. It might even be a vacation—because you've earned it!

And if your perfect day means working in your business, making the donuts, or polishing teeth, that's absolutely okay. I just want you to have the choice. Every process in your business must run whether you're in the building or not, and that means abdication of operations.

Abdication represents the opportunity for fulfillment. For the first time, the entrepreneur has more money than she needs. She has time freedom. She has opportunity. Each of those brings new challenges, but as entrepreneurs are fond of saying, "These are the right problems to have." But remember: no abdication without automation. Whatever your next pursuit, the golden goose must keep laying. Your cash machine must keep producing without your involvement. If you're always taking calls from your first salon, you'll never be able to open a second.

THE TINKER'S #HASHTAG

A tinker has built a business that runs itself. Now she's trying to build another, to duplicate her first success, to take her first idea to a new market, or to start over with a new idea. The tinker's defining hashtags are #focus, #leadership, and #perfectday.

I've never met a tinker who didn't have at least three big projects in mind. Free from their original business—and still making passive income from it—the tinker has more options than time. If she's not given new challenges, the tinker will probably stick her hands in the machine, constantly "tweaking" her original business until it's broken.

When nonentrepreneurs picture a company founder, they're usually picturing a tinker. But most entrepreneurs never actually make it to that point. Most wind up buying themselves a job (Founder phase) or working in the business at all hours, taking a little profit and fighting the good fight forever (Farmer phase). There's nothing wrong with either. What's important is that you have the choice.

Many people are happy in their vocation: they love coaching fitness, or they love cutting hair, or they love making beautiful smiles in their dental practice. But some want more.

The tinkers in Two-Brain Business are turning their businesses into franchises, developing online projects, partnering with other owners, and starting second companies. Others are setting up their retirement plans and buying buildings to create cash flow assets. My role as their mentor is to help them identify the next big project and then keep them focused on it.

THE TINKER'S VALUES

In the Founder phase, the new entrepreneur recorded their unimpeachable values and where they were learned. In the Farmer phase, the entrepreneur taught those values to their team. But by the time a founder becomes a tinker, the company has learned its own lessons. Services have evolved. "Weed" clients have been removed, and "apple" clients have been cultivated. The company's needs have also changed. Where the founder opened a business to secure herself a job, the company now has a responsibility to its workers, its neighbors, and its clients.

If you plan to step away from day-to-day operations, you better make sure your staff completely buys into the company's mission, vision, and values. And complete buy-in means staff must have some skin in the game: they must play a larger role in shaping the company's values.

The team needs to recreate its values to reflect the current state of the business along with setting the business up for future decisions and planning, and they need to do it themselves with as little steering from you as you can muster. Make space for them to see themselves reflected in the company's culture, values, and goals. Doing so will unite your team members to work toward your shared mission, whether or not you're in the room.

THE TINKER'S KINGMAKER EQUATION

Your Kingmaker goal in the Tinker phase is an EHR of $500 per hour. That's the EHR required to create $1,000,000 in value for the business each year.

A tinker should introduce a management layer into their company, comprised of specialists focused on operations, sales, and financial planning. When assigning a value to each role in your company, note the roles in which you can be replaced for less than $500 per hour. Then replace yourself in those roles and leverage that time to work on higher-value functions that create more than $500 for the business for every hour spent.

If you can't find tasks that will create more than $500 per hour in value to your company, focus on partnerships, sales, and new revenue streams. Of course, the other side of the equation is time spent: you could just cut down your hours worked to drive up their Kingmaker equation. As a tinker, the choice is yours.

THE TINKER'S INCOME GOAL

Robert Kiyosaki's *Rich Dad, Poor Dad* changed the way I

thought about my future, retirement, and money. Before reading it, I thought that I'd contribute to a retirement savings plan. Maybe I'd go wild and buy a few stocks. But Kiyosaki introduced me to cash flow assets: things you own that PAY you and don't stop.

Kiyosaki's story is mostly about real estate. He would like readers to purchase a building, then rent it to someone else, generating a stream of revenue that should last for decades. But he also made me comfortable using borrowed money to finance my big ideas. And he triggered the huge question that has been my muse ever since: Can a business be a true cash flow asset? In other words, could a business ever operate without any guidance from me? Could it run—profitably—on autopilot? What systems would I need to build for that to happen?

Tim Ferriss' excellent book *The 4-Hour Workweek* encouraged me in this quest. A four-hour workweek seemed extreme at the time—and he later admitted that the number was chosen for shock value—but I wanted to go even further: I wanted to go to ZERO. I wanted my high-touch service business (a gym) to run without my presence or attention. And I had huge motivation to do so: I was writing two books. I was mentoring other gym owners, and I wanted to show just how far someone could go.

Of course, automating a relationship business was

tough. But here's the process (which, by now, should look familiar).

Break down your roles and tasks. Think of the hats you still wear in your business (those you have not yet automated or assigned to someone else): bookkeeper, web designer...After breaking down all the roles, assign tasks to each one.

Create gold standards for each role. You don't want "acceptable" completion; you want the relentless pursuit of excellence. Your staff should compare themselves to the best in the world, not the best among them.

Create an evaluation scale, working backward from the gold standard. If "best in class" is a ten out of ten, what's a nine? Explain each level, and use illustrations and examples as much as possible. Then schedule evaluation periods and criteria so your staff knows exactly how to be excellent.

Do a time valuation. Assign a dollar value to each role based on the cost to replace you in that role.

Work toward removing yourself from ALL roles. That's the point we call "retirement." The other huge lesson I got from Kiyosaki was this: If cash flow without time commitment equals retirement, why can't we all just retire *now*?

Ferriss complemented this idea with his own "mini-retirements," taken through life in short spans of a few months. Retire to Brazil, for example, while you're young enough to enjoy it and then return to Manhattan six months later. This approach is a great test for every business. For a company to be scalable or salable, it must operate without its founder for as long as possible. And the only way to really assess the value of your company is to test its ability to stay afloat while you work on other projects. To that end, we assign a secret "test" period for all founders in our Incubator program: go away for five days without email or phone connection to your business. Then, when you return, patch up the holes and test again.

Think about the relative value of a business that requires constant care versus a business that needs no oversight. The latter is a cash flow asset, an automated business that allows its owner to do anything—start another company, research cryptocurrency—or do nothing. THAT is retirement. But before you give yourself a gold watch, you need to test your systems. Retirement from your business means no longer delegating but abdicating. Your staff must make every single decision without you. Are you comfortable with letting them make decisions? Are you willing to stake the rest of your life on it, even if you live another hundred years?

My first exposure to a real entrepreneur was in high

school. J. J. Hilsinger was a lifelong entrepreneur who got his start by selling chickens out of his trunk. Those profits turned into a restaurant, then J. J. bought the hotel behind the restaurant, then he bought a ski resort. My teacher invited him to speak to our advanced business class.

J. J. showed up five minutes late, gray ponytail flying behind him. He didn't have any notes and instead just looked at the audience and said, "Raise your hand if you're going to live to a hundred." Almost every hand shot into the air. We were young and bulletproof.

Then he said, "Raise your hand if you're going to live to a hundred and twenty-five." I dropped mine, but some of the really overconfident science nerds kept theirs aloft.

Then he said, "Keep your hand up if you're going to live to a hundred and fifty." Only his remained.

"Two hundred?" J. J.'s hand stayed up. Most of the kids stopped paying attention because this hippie was clearly nuts. I don't remember the rest of the speech. But that question—asked thirty years ago—doesn't seem so ridiculous now.

In a room full of thirty-to-fifty-year-old millionaires, most of us with a high degree of physical fitness, Dan Martell posed a similar question, "Who thinks they're going to die before they reach 125?" No one raised a hand. He followed up with, "Let me rephrase. Who's going to live to 150?" And over half the room—brilliant people—responded that they expected to reach 150. That's incredible. Thirty years ago, most people thought a 150-year lifespan was an absurd idea. Now many scientists and doctors agree that the first person to reach 150 is probably already walking among us.

Why does this matter to entrepreneurs?

It means that most of us have a very long way to go. We're not going to retire at sixty and sit on the couch for ninety more years. And we're probably not going to own the same business in ninety years. (When J. J. asked that question of my high school business class, the internet didn't exist, and no one had a portable phone.) We were all still in the bottom of the first inning.

To retire with an antifragile portfolio, you'll need a variety of assets that generate cash without your constant supervision. Your business can be one. Others might come from rental properties, mutual funds, index funds, or a variety of financial plans. So what's your target age? How will entrepreneurship change the way you view "retirement"? How will an extra twenty-five years make you think about your fitness today?

CORE CONCEPT: THE FLOW STATE: THINKING BODY, DANCING MIND

The "flow" state occurs when you're totally immersed in a task. You become focused and optimally productive. While in flow state, the body moves automatically, requiring very little conscious thought. Its preoccupation with repetitive movement "frees" the mind to wander or focus. "Flow" is harder to achieve while sitting still, except for those educated in mindfulness practice. But for novices (like me), a shortcut to total mental immersion is repetitive physical work.

In *Thinking Body, Dancing Mind*, author Chungliang Al Huang discusses the path to "flow state" through mindfulness training and yoga (which originated as physical exercise to prepare the body for long periods of meditation). I prefer a more down-to-earth method: a big pile of dirt.

Years ago, when my business was faltering, my wife bought me a truckload of dirt. I didn't have the money to pay a builder, so I tasked myself with leveling our driveway. It was hard work, done in small increments on my rare time off. But as I worked, I considered different options for restructuring my business. As the weeks passed, I became eager to "hit the dirt" on Sunday afternoons after the gym closed. In fact, I felt guilty about spending time with the dirt pile instead of my daughter. I was enjoying it so much!

When our son's hockey team failed to secure ice time for practices, I saw the chance for another pile of dirt and volunteered to enlarge the rink in our backyard. Relatives asked why I chose to shovel the dirt into place myself instead of using a tractor, which was readily available. I consider the opportunity for physical labor a luxury. It's recreational time for my brain. The pile of pit-run gravel requires just enough focus to block out distractions.

You don't need a giant pile of dirt to enter a "flow" state, of course. Simple labor around the house will do the trick. Walking is enough for some, but if you add external load (a weighted pack) to the task, you'll have to work a bit harder physically and your mind will be free to focus. Mark Divine, author of *Unbeatable Mind* and *Way of the SEAL*, explained the flow state to me this way:

> Flow comes when you have a high degree of competence that meets a slightly higher degree of challenge. When you're really striving for something that you're good at, then you tend to lock into a flow state when the challenge starts to slightly exceed your skill level. It's experienced as a manipulation of time of getting out of your thinking, rational mind and having a high degree of competence, just

literally flow out of you. That's where the term "flow" came from. We call it unconscious competence.

The flow state presents an interesting paradigm: on the one hand, the body must be performing a task for which it has been well prepared; on the other, the task must not be TOO challenging, or the brain will be required for conscious consideration of each movement. It's necessary for the central and peripheral nervous systems to remain alert while the brain relaxes. That's why repetitive work, simple exercise, or holding a familiar-but-challenging static posture works so well. Divine continued:

> Let's say you are surfing a wave, and you're just like, "This is amazing." You know you've got the skills, you're on the wave, you don't have to think about the wave, and you don't have to think about your position on the board. Your body is just reacting and responding intuitively, naturally. That's the experience of the flow state.

He brings up an essential point: for flow to occur, there must be stimulation of the nervous system, even as the brain frees itself from the constraints of consciousness. The tricky part, however, is allowing the brain to actually be free.

Frequently, we're bogged down with negative thoughts, checklists, or other attention drainers that require too much conscious effort without physical effort being involved. For example, think about the dishes waiting for you in your sink. Perhaps a date is coming over after work, and you're worried that you won't have time to clean your kitchen before she arrives. Though the work is simple— you've done it hundreds of times—it's distracting because the importance attributed to the task far outweighs the action required to complete it.

For the full workday, you think about your sink full of dishes waiting at home; strategize ways to leave work quickly, or even early, to get them done; consider other options (inviting her out to eat); and you'll even dwell over worst-case scenarios. These tiny, day-to-day distractions, which may take little effort but can't be immediately resolved, build up into a logjam that prevents "flow."

Negative emotions are the largest culprits here, since your brain is hardwired to focus on threats and emotional responses to problems rather than resolutions. It's much easier to put aside a happy memory from the weekend and "get down to work" than it is to forget your daughter's crying before school that morning, for instance. If you're a manager, anger at an employee who's frequently late or messy may hinder your ability to do your own work.

In these cases, having a tried and true method for getting into flow will do you a world of good. Divine agrees:

"There is a skill of entering the flow state that can be trained and mastered, which will allow you to enter it at will." Whether it is a pile of dirt, a long run, or vacuuming your living room, figure out the methods and conditions that work best for you and make the flow state a regular practice. Take Mark Divine's advice and treat flow as a skill to be mastered.

THE TINKER'S TIME GOAL

Work expands to fill the space you give it. You know that by now.

It's easy to spend a day being "busy" but accomplishing little. Small tasks are always available to fill your time, and rabbit holes like chatting up visitors and Facebook groups can drag you in for hours. Just like budgeting your money, scheduling your time can help you optimize your efforts. You're a tinker now, and you will succeed by focusing your attention, limiting your tasks, and optimizing your time.

HOW TO OPTIMIZE YOUR DAY

First, you're going to create two windows for uninterrupted work. The first work window is for checklists; the second is for creativity.

First window: FOCUS. Pull up your checklist for the day.

Find the simplest task to perform and work it through to completion. Then find the next simplest and work it all the way through. This is single-tasking. But it's also using the cognitive tendency called gap theory to get you some momentum and draw you into the "flow state," where you work at your optimum focused pace.

During your focus window, you need to be in a quiet place with a door that closes. You also need to turn off your phone and desktop notifications. If you work better with music, play some. If you don't, don't. (I work best in complete silence.)

As you work through your list, cross the completed tasks off and add them to your "Done" list. At the end of your focus window, you'll want to see what you've accomplished. That's important. If you have trouble getting started, use the Hemingway hack: start with something that's almost done already. Hemingway would stop writing midsentence at the end of each day so the next morning he could merely finish the sentence and then be in a flow state.

Second window: CREATE. During this block, you're going to do more creative work. This window is when you post your social media stuff, write your blog posts, or film your videos. It's also when you create the next day's checklist. Your creative time is more free-flowing but absolutely necessary. It's not nap time. You still have to build.

Many entrepreneurs find they think best when their body is occupied with a repetitive task. So if you have trouble coming up with a blog topic, go mow the grass or head out for a walk. You can't hit a CrossFit workout and call it your "creative" time, though, because hard workouts require too much conscious attention.

You can also use tools like 750words.com to urge you through creative work, or practice games like Tabata Talking, which we teach entrepreneurs.

Target Your Peak Cognitive Windows. Abe Lincoln said, "Give me six hours to chop down a tree, and I will spend the first four sharpening the ax." An entrepreneur's greatest tool is his brain, but most of us never sharpen that tool. Instead of improving our cognition, focus, and memory, we try to use the same dull edge to cut larger and larger trees. We can do cognitive exercises (found online at TwoBrain.com/flow) or use physical activity to create peak cognitive performance.

Focus time is best done before the day starts or after a hard mental reset. For me, that means a 4 a.m. start before anyone else is awake. I start with the easy stuff: doing money transfers and processing payments from the night before. Then I do responsive stuff: answering emails and messages. That's my segue into creative time when I write blog posts and love letters to my email list.

Because most of my work is creative, my "focus" time usually involves building or optimizing materials that will help business owners—work that is, by nature, creative but not free-flow writing.

If you're not an early morning person, that's fine. Try to schedule your focus window to immediately follow a hard workout. Tough workouts, like CrossFit, require your full attention, which temporarily blocks out little distractions. That creates a short time frame in which you can follow the focus window directions above (notifications off, doors closed). You'll need at least one hour per day of focus time, with a plan to build to two or more eventually.

Creative time is optimized by low-level exercise or a menial task. I have my best ideas while splitting wood or shoveling dirt. The challenge with these outdoor activities is that I rarely have a notepad around when I have my ideas. Ditto for driving and showering.

If you can find a menial task—like mopping the floors of your business or rearranging boxes in your supply room—that keeps you close to a laptop, this is often best: you can go back and forth between doing the work and recording your ideas. Low-level aerobic stimulation, like walking, can help you remember facts more quickly AND make connections between ideas faster.

These practices are just that: practices. You won't be great on your first day. Each is its own fitness, which means they're both trainable, and improving both is critical for business owners.

THE TINKER'S BRAND

I have a dentist. She's been my dentist for a decade, and in those ten years, she has moved her practice three times. And I've followed her because my relationship is with her, not her office. Obviously, this is great for her—she'll be my dentist for life—but it's *not* great for the dental offices she leaves.

I have a financial advisor. He has a "book of business" with my name in it and knows that I prefer index funds to RSPs and real estate over any paper investment. I'll go with him if he moves his practice to another company, and I imagine many of his clients would too. This is great news for him, obviously, but it's *not* great for his office.

Regardless of whether your plan is to become a better CEO or abdicate the position, your company's brand must take on its own identity. Your clients need to have a relationship with your brand that overrides their relationship with any specific staff person.

Establishing your brand's identity independent of you or your staff starts with your clients. If you don't want your book of business to follow members of your team down the street, you have to take a different approach to keep your brand in the forefront of your clients' minds. Here's how:

- Change your lexicon. Avoid staff references to "my client" and "your client." Instead, refer to "the team" and "our client," and use "we" in your correspondence.
- Regularly switch staff around for your clients.
- Use vacations and days off to introduce new staff to your clients.
- Put the best person in each role. If one bookkeeper is bad at sending birthday cards or congratulating clients, the client suffers. But if you have one amazing staff person in the role of congratulation and retention, it solidifies the relationship between your accounting practice and the client.
- Sign correspondence with "Your friends at Catalyst" instead of "Chris."
- Tell staff to keep communication lines with clients professional. Don't give out personal cell phone numbers or personal email addresses. There's a strong

legal reason for this too. If a client ever tried to sue the business, the staff member's personal text and email history could become the property of the plaintiff if they're using it with the client. And really, who *wants* a client texting them at 4 a.m.?

- Encourage all staff to establish their authority outside of their client sessions by producing educational videos and blog posts. Make THEM famous.

- Hire a diverse array of staff. I love to say, "I want you to train with Mike for the next three months. He's great at accountability. Then you can move back to Bill in September when you're getting ready for ski season again."

- Don't depend on nonsales staff for sales. If they're the client's only point of contact, the client will follow them wherever they go. Do goal reviews, or have a separate staff specialist meeting with the client three times per year.

- In general, expose every client to at least three different members of your staff.

You got the clients. You signed them up. You paid for your website and painted your office. You're also doing your best to provide meaningful careers for your coaches. But if it doesn't work out, do you lose the kids in the divorce? Of course not. And that's why building loyalty to the brand is so essential. The above approaches will go a long way to deepening client loyalty, but you can't stop there. You need to expand it as well.

PRODUCTIZING YOUR SERVICE

An emerging trend in the service industry is to "pro-ductize" your service—to create reproducibility to drive costs down and increase volume. For example, instead of delivering the same lecture ten times for $100 each appearance, a teacher could record his talk once and sell it a hundred times for $10, netting the same revenue for one-tenth the work. Kim Ki-hoon, an English teacher in South Korea, does this very thing. His net income in 2014 was over four million dollars, according to the *Wall Street Journal*.

In my own practice, after working one-on-one with over two thousand entrepreneurs, I've found that everyone can benefit from a basic curriculum. Then, because every business has its own unique fingerprint, I include a few one-on-one calls to tailor the program to their specific needs.

While one-on-one attention is critical to success, the combination of video and personal teaching creates the opportunity to deliver my consulting to more entre-preneurs at a lower price. I can help more people. Some still prefer one-on-one guidance through the whole process, and that's fine, but for the more adventurous do-it-yourself entrepreneur, I can allow them to prog-ress at their own pace outside of my schedule and then help when they become stuck. It's a great way to build momentum, and I love it. Best of all, it allows Two-Brain Business to reach entrepreneurs who might've otherwise never heard about us, and those who couldn't afford one-on-one mentoring. We still get to help them win.

There are other opportunities in the service industry (for example, a financial planner could send out a series of videos guiding clients toward different options for life insurance, retirement savings, etc.), but care should be taken. There's no such thing as one-size-fits-all for most of your clients, and many services can't be productized. Clients can learn how to apply lipstick but not cut their own hair. Not everyone likes their steak cooked the same way. If you productize a system completely, it can't provide a perfect solution.

And with that comes another warning: turning your service entirely into a product opens the door for commodity pricing. When two products are the same, they compete on price. Delivering a one-size-fits-all option or turning your service into a product opens the door to commoditization. If all else is equal in the mind of the client, the price will be the differentiator.

The bottom line: productizing your service is a great way to expand brand awareness and build loyalty among new audiences, BUT your product must be infused with the same things that make your service great: your values, gold standards, and the high level of service you deliver every day.

THE TINKER'S SALES AND MARKETING PLAN

In the founder and Farmer phases, the owner of the business wore the sales hat out of necessity. She used Affinity Marketing right from the start and gradually expanded her influence through personal contact, then an email list, and then a funnel. But you're a tinker now, and you must outsource sales and marketing.

Of the three meta roles, which we will discuss shortly, the sales chair is hardest to vacate. It's relatively easy to appoint someone else as CFO because most business owners don't get excited about spreadsheets and financial projections. It's harder to remove yourself from daily operations, but the steps to do so are clear (and laid out in Part Two, "Farmer"). Appointing a staff person to oversee operations or take the COO gauntlet is merely a matter of optimizing everything in the business and having it work without your input. As you learned, the process takes time, but the hard work of roles and tasks and playbooks was motivating. But sales are different. The sales role touches the client AND the money.

Many entrepreneurs still wrestle with the icon problem in the Tinker phase: "But my clients are really buying ME!"

They might also be reluctant to share revenue data or sales data with their staff. But at this level, radical transparency is necessary for all processes. You can't afford to have a left hand that doesn't know what the right is doing. That means putting one person in charge of sales and marketing. Their job is to assist in the development of the sales plan and then fulfill that plan.

The tinker vacates the sales seat the same way the founder relinquished their first low-value role: by recording the process (leaving tracks), then testing the process under someone else's hand and evaluating performance over time. While the metrics measured for the sales chair might be vastly different than those measured for cleaning the floors, the process can scale up to any level.

FIRST, BUILD YOUR PLAN

The first step to filling the sales chair is to build an annual sales and marketing plan. At Two-Brain Business, we use a circle chart and the "rocks in a glass" analogy to plan our sales and marketing calendar.

In case you're not familiar with the analogy, you fill a glass by first adding your big rocks, then by adding your pebbles, then sifting sand into the pebbles, and finally by adding water to fill the microscopic spaces between the sand. If you start with the water first, you'll never have space for the big, important rocks because the glass will already be full.

The analogy is useful for describing how to invest your time (plan for your family first, then your health, then your business), your money (buy your buildings, then your mutual funds, then your index funds, then a savings account perhaps) or your energy. It's especially useful when talking about marketing because small daily practices can easily fill all of your marketing time and budget without creating a noticeable effect.

Start by scheduling your big endeavors (the 'rocks' in the glass): product launches, events, product combinations, or upgrade releases. They might not fit into a regular quarterly schedule, but place them on your circle chart like this:

For example, Two-Brain Business releases an updated Incubator program every January, and entrepreneurs flock to it. By mid-March, most of the entrepreneurs will upgrade to the next stage of mentorship to keep their momentum going. Our annual summit is usually in June, and by mid-September, we package up our summit videos with our Incubator program as a special bonus to entrepreneurs.

The next step is the "pebbles" step: to fill in the primary marketing activities that will support the "rocks." These could be your launch plan for a new product or your invitation to an event. It could be outbound calls to previous clients, or even the eight-word email your studio sends to people on your list. If your goal is conversion to a higher-value service, goal reviews (or client meetings) could be your best bet.

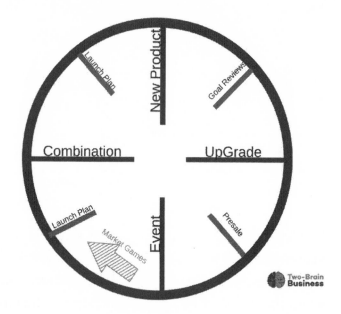

The third step is to place the "sand" in the glass: the everyday marketing strategies that can be tailored toward your "big project" or done as a recurring funnel activity. For example, many entrepreneurs now run Facebook ads all the time, but they might alter them every few weeks to retarget an audience or promote a different service. Others might publish daily blog posts or YouTube videos but tailor their content to lead up to their big project. This is also the level at which you plan lead magnets, webinars, or other short-term digital strategies.

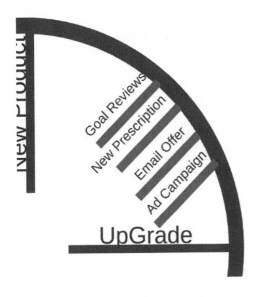

Finally, some sales and marketing tactics should be done every single day. One of the corporate examples I cite in this book is CrossFit, the fastest-growing exercise network on the planet. Beginning in 2001, CrossFit founder Greg Glassman posted a "Workout of the Day" (WOD) every single day on CrossFit.com. When social media began its rise, the practice began to yield exponential results. And when I attended a CrossFit Media Summit in 2013, then-director Tony Budding told me, "We publish every single day. No exceptions."

By that point, CrossFit Inc. was producing daily videos, blog posts, and pictures, along with their WODs. Their media team was growing rapidly, and they were soon able to produce full-length feature documentaries and movies. If you visit CrossFit, Inc.'s Facebook page today and look at its service description, you'll notice that CrossFit lists itself as a "media company," not a fitness brand. Content marketing is THAT important.

Like CrossFit, I've personally published a blog post almost every day since 2012. But any kind of relevant content will work, as long as it leads back to your funnel. The point is to fill in those tiny gaps. Content marketing is the "water" that fills in all the gaps between the grains of sand.

FIND YOUR METRICS

The next step in hiring a sales chair is to decide which metrics to measure. Facebook's Ads Manager alone has dozens of possible metrics to watch. But we teach entrepreneurs to measure five important sales metrics:

- Leads
- Appointments booked
- Appointments attended
- Conversions
- Lifetime value (determined by measuring their ARM by their LEG, and explained further in the Founder section)

A sales manager's role is to improve all of those metrics, but conversion is most important. While a good retention plan will vastly improve lifetime value, retention sits under the COO's purview. The chief sales officer should measure success in conversions and use the other metrics to determine how their strategy is working.

DECIDE ON A COMPENSATION STRUCTURE

Sales staff, especially outbound sales, are usually paid on commission or on a combination of base wage plus commission. The CSO should benefit financially from the upside of their work; the entrepreneur should minimize the risk by setting the base pay rate low and commission level high.

In product-based companies, this commission structure could even be as high as 50 percent of gross sales, because the first salesman in the company determines the sales template for everyone else to follow. The next salesman would make a much smaller percentage. In service-based companies, the commission would be much lower because initial purchase value would be higher and margins lower. We recommend a flat rate per conversion that's equal to or less than 8.5 percent of annual client value (or, if it's easier, the equivalent of one month's revenue from the client).

If your LEG is under twelve months, pay a commission of 8.5 percent of lifetime value. If LEG is over twelve months, pay a commission of 8.5 percent of the value of one year. The CFO will help you determine what you can afford to pay to acquire each client.

As with any other role, test your process for a fixed term. Hire subjectively but measure objectively. Choose the applicant with the best personality, but keep the staff with the best performance metrics over time. With the sales role taken care of, you can shift your focus to filling out the rest of your company's managerial meta roles.

THE TINKER'S ROLES

The goal of the Tinker phase is to free the entrepreneur from the primary business. This means continuing to function as the CEO (for now), but introducing a managerial layer of "meta roles": a COO, CFO, and CSO.

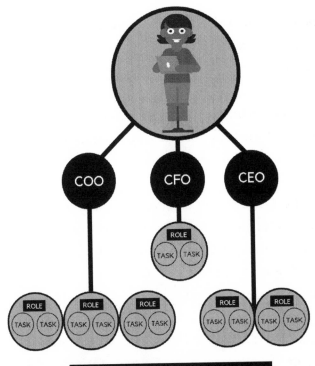

TINKER PHASE HIERARCHY

THE META ROLES

The first homework I received from a mentor was to "break down the roles in my business." I was assigned *The E-Myth* by Michael Gerber and spent one boring weekend breaking down all the roles in my gym (about twelve back then, now about eighteen) and then assigning tasks to each role (about twelve to each, again). I wish I had known that there are really three META roles that oversee everything else.

I like to visualize three chairs high on Mount Olympus. They look like directors' chairs with a word written on the back of each:

- **Finance:** The person who tracks your revenues and expenses, forecasts the future of each, and advises action based on numbers. The accountant and financial planner.
- **Sales/Marketing:** The person who oversees the negotiation of sales (integration) and generates awareness/interest. The ads manager, newsletter writer, content creator.
- **Operations:** The person who oversees the delivery of your service. The general manager.

YOU get to sit in one of these chairs but ONLY one. And that means going to zero in the other two.

It starts with processes, of course. You can't "level up" from any role until you've entirely replaced yourself in that role, but these meta roles require a bit more.

As a tinker, you need someone to lead, manage, and be accountable for (LMA) each role. Gino Wickman discusses the idea in depth in his book *Traction*—another recommended read.

A service business run by an owner-operator can scale to a

considerable level using the Roles and Tasks and Valuing Your Time lessons in the Founder and Farmer sections, but when a company is going to scale quickly—maybe by selling an online service or product—you must replace yourself in two of these meta roles as early as possible.

BEWARE THE "VALLEY OF DEATH"

When entrepreneurs reach the Tinker phase, they commonly refer to the "valley of death," the point where their company is growing incrementally but their costs are increasing exponentially. For the first time, they're hiring from outside their company and probably recruiting a skillset that they don't possess themselves. They're hiring more expensive roles than ever before or adding capacity they aren't confident they can fill. It's a scary period.

But we can use Michalowicz's *Profit First* strategy to test these new costs:

- Create a new account for the position or new expense you'd like to hire.
- Write checks to that account for three months in advance.
- Take them to the bank and deposit them. Get them out of sight.

How well does the business survive? Was the cost noticeable, or did you merely absorb it? Did you ramp up production or sales to meet the new expense?

If not, rethink your strategy. But if you've just proven that you can afford the new meta role, hire them fast and get ready to lead.

HOW TO LEAD

The larger the business, the larger the leadership skill-set required. Many entrepreneurs replace themselves in the CEO role; others struggle to "level up" to this new responsibility. In the effort to be a better mentor, I study leadership a lot. I learn from my own mentors, read the biographies of leaders, and listen to their words while training or driving my truck. Here are the things common to successful leaders:

1. They model the behavior they want from others.
2. They give clear directions, with no missing steps.
3. They fall back on daily routines.
4. They make a lot of mistakes but never the same one twice.
5. They're not confident all the time but know it's more important to appear confident than ambivalent.
6. They create other leaders.

Let's examine the first two traits a bit deeper.

1. Modeling

In college, I had a nutrition professor who was a walking textbook. She could recite data and draw tables about glycemic load and macronutrient profiles. But she also ate McDonald's in her office after class. I can't recall a single lecture she gave, but I can recall the smell of her desk area perfectly.

This is sometimes an inconvenient truth, but "Do as I say, not as I do" is ineffective. If you're a parent, you already know it won't work. But it's easy to fool yourself into believing your staff (even the high-level ones) don't care about what YOU do.

If you're a hairdresser, your hair should look great every day.

If you're a personal trainer, you should work out.

If you're selling stocks and bonds, you should wear something expensive.

Your staff will follow the example you set at your worst. Your adherence to your own rules will cue them to follow. If you break your own rules occasionally, they'll break them often. Your lowest standard of care will become their best standard of care because, after all, that's what you show them. You are the example, not the exception.

For example, my gym has a "back door" we don't want clients to use. Clients should use the front door, where the check-in kiosk sits. But the back door is close to the parking lot, and one day I slipped out back to grab my wallet from my truck. Another coach saw me do it, and despite my instructions to never use the door, she began to use it as her main entrance. The door has a "Do Not Enter" sign on it. Our staff handbook tells our coaches to park in back and enter through the front. But she saw ME do it, and that made it okay. You can guess what happened next: clients saw her using it and started to do the same.

If your accountant's desk is crammed with loose paper and receipts, will you show up at the tax deadline with a shoebox crammed full of random paper? Of course, because you think it's okay. After all, your model of book-keeping responsibility does it this way.

2. Set the Mission

Create a clear, simple goal for your business. This goal must tell a story, be clear, and be repeatable by your staff. For example, Two-Brain Business's mission is to make 1,000,000 entrepreneurs wealthy. That's easy to remember and easy for staff to repeat. If your staff doesn't understand the mission or can't repeat it without strug-gling, it's not effective.

At the tinker level, staff can't ask questions about every recurring task. They need to be able to hold their questions up against your corporate mission and ask, "Does this fit?" The clearer your mission, the easier that answer will be. Repeat your mission at every single opportunity. Let your mission be the North Star that guides the daily decisions in your business.

3. Teach the Vision

What will success look like? Paint that picture for your staff.

In the Founder phase, entrepreneurs paint a picture of their "perfect day" to create a vision of success for themselves. In the Farmer phase, entrepreneurs ask their staff to envision their own perfect days, and help them create a roadmap to that point. In the Tinker phase, success means accomplishing the mission. What will the world look like if the mission is successful? What will success mean to your clients and your community?

The vision must anchor your company's "why" to its "how." For example, Two-Brain Business's mission is to make 1,000,000 entrepreneurs wealthy. As the world economy evolves from agricultural/industrial to idea/tech, entrepreneurs will buoy the new economy with their businesses. And as the internet decentralizes production, anyone with a great idea can start a business. We want those businesses to be successful. We want to create jobs, meaningful lives, and wealth for those willing to take a risk. We want healthy economies, healthy business owners, and healthy families. We want the people on the front lines doing innovative work in healthcare and the environment to succeed against those who would stop them.

Who will save our economy? The entrepreneur. Our mission is to make those entrepreneurs successful in THEIR mission. And the vision we teach our team is that of global impact through local success.

4. Map the Journey

Beginning with the vision in mind, work backward to map the journey. Start with a ten-year horizon on your mission. Then break it up into annual steps.

If we want to make 1,000,000 entrepreneurs wealthy in ten years, that's 100,000 entrepreneurs per year.

That's 8,300 entrepreneurs per month, or around 276 per day.

How can we serve 276 entrepreneurs per day?

Define your metrics for success: How will we define "service"? How will we define customer success? Teach those metrics to your staff.

5. Talk to Your People

Repeat your mission and vision over and over to your staff. As I've learned (the hard way), the leader of a growing company must devote as much time talking to his team as to his customers.

Has this happened to you?

"Hey, Chris, a client just asked me about the new X program. Uh, what exactly IS that?"

"Hey, Chris, a client just read something on our website and asked me about it. I'd never heard it before, so I thought I'd ask you before responding."

"Hey, Chris, a couple of the other guys on the team were curious about..."

Then you smack your head and wonder, "How can they NOT KNOW THIS?"

Smack yourself twice because you already know the

answer. You haven't told them. At least, not well enough or often enough or clearly enough.

Speaking with Marco Zappacosta, cofounder of Thumbtack.com, I learned that I was shouting too much in one direction and not enough in another. Think about all the media you produce for your clients: blog posts, videos, social media, podcasts. How much do you produce for your staff?

Think about the care and quality you put into your client-facing media: editing, producing, scripting, and polishing. How much do you think about the messages to your team?

Think about the brand you present to the outside world: the clarity, the repeatability, and the stickiness. How many stories do you share with those following behind you on the path?

Here's your recipe for good media balance:

In the Founder phase, aim your bullhorn outward. You're doing most of the work. The company's vision is YOUR vision. Make your clients famous; share your story; publish every day. Meet strangers. Teach the benefit of your service. If you have any staff, you see them every single day. Talk to them about your plans, but you don't need to send a daily blog post to your wife.

Outward-facing media: 100 percent. Inward-facing media: 0 percent.

In the Farmer phase, you're adding staff and revenue diversity. You need to establish a clear North Star: a simple, repeatable, sticky mission. You need to talk to future clients more than ever, but you also need to make sure your staff knows everything that's happening. Diversify your media for clients *and* staff. Add channels. Use YouTube and email, for example, but publish less frequently. Twice per week for staff-facing media is good.

Outward-facing media: 80 percent. Inward-facing media: 20 percent.

In the Tinker phase, the leader of the company isn't involved in daily operations. That means less chatter while unloading the dishwasher and fewer in-person interactions with your staff. Your outward-facing media channels should be diverse and appeal to anyone willing to pay attention. Post videos on YouTube, pull the audio, and publish it as a podcast. Transcribe the audio into blog posts. Send the blog posts to your email lists. Share snippets on social. Then do the same for your staff. Just as your clients won't always read your emails, your staff might prefer an audio update to a video or text one.

Outward-facing media: 50 percent. Inward-facing media: 50 percent.

One tip Zappacosta shared: recording a daily voice message and texting it to every single employee in his company. They can listen to it on their way to work. But don't forget the love letters and videos!

Your total media output should grow as your company grows. But as it does, make sure to grow both sides of the media tree instead of leaving a bare patch against the wall.

6. Evaluate Success

Sharing your mission and vision with your staff is simple. Simply repeat both at every opportunity. But sharing responsibility with your staff is tough. Your ego gets in the way. ("No one can do this as well as I can!") Your budget gets in the way. ("I can just do this myself and keep the money!") And even your watch gets in the way. ("It takes them twice as long to do the job!")

You know you need to leverage your time to achieve your EHR goal. But it's hard to keep your fingers out of the machine, isn't it? Here's how to guide your staff to deliver the gold standard in their role so you can work on growing your business:

Founder phase: Take your Roles and Tasks sheet, and apply a scale of 1 to 10 to each task. Every three months, book a staff evaluation with each person, and review the tasks on their sheet. Score them from 1 to 10, and then highlight their bright spots and opportunities for growth.

Farmer phase: Sit with each of your staff every quarter. Ask them to redo their Perfect Day exercise and then review their goals using our career roadmap tool. Then get into the nitty-gritty parts. Ask them to review themselves at each task using the evaluation scale above. Compare their answers to your own. Ask them how you can help them improve.

Tinker phase: At this stage, it's no longer enough to have people check boxes like cogs in a machine. Your process problems have been resolved, and your role now is to lead people. This means putting the right people in the right seats. Start by delivering a clear vision of your mission to your staff. Then use personality assessments to make sure your key staff are in the right roles. Next, measure the effect of your service through client surveys and discussions, and deliver that feedback to your leadership team. Have them carry your mission to your staff and evaluate their progress, as above. But adding a layer of external quality control is absolutely essential; otherwise, you'll walk around your business looking for problems instead of going outside and looking for opportunities.

When you reach the Thief phase, you'll sit with your CEO and ask, "What problems do you have, and how can I help you solve them?" Your purpose will simply be to build the renown of your brand (both business and personal). The CEO should have reports created by an independent source, like a quality control company.

Your goals don't change as your business grows, but your leverage does. Your ability to impact more people depends on your growth as a leader. You must share your mission with your team, you must evolve your brand strategy, and you must also evolve your evaluation process.

LEAVING A FARMER BEHIND

When tinkers test their business and discover they CAN take two months off with full income, they know it's time to start the next one. They decide which big idea to pursue and then dive in with the enthusiasm of a founder all over again. These are heady times. The rush of novelty makes you feel young again, and the feeling that "I can't lose this time!" just adds wind to your wings. But many would-be abdicators get brought back to earth *hard*.

A client texts about a bad experience, or a once-in-a-lifetime circumstance threatens to kill the golden goose. They're immediately distracted away from their higher-level project and pulled back into their original business.

It's a struggle I'm all too familiar with. When I visited my gym last week, I walked into a reception area and immediately noticed a coach's lunch spread all over the welcome desk. I saw a burned-out light bulb. And I heard silence. Where was the music? These are tiny things. A client might never notice. But I did, and it ruined my mindset for the rest of the day. Every business needs a farmer, and if it's not someone else, it's you. When the time comes to replace yourself in your primary business, you have to leave a farmer in control.

This means granting (and paying for) a layer of responsibility that goes beyond completing a task list. The farmer you hire needs the ability to make decisions and probably make a few mistakes. She needs the freedom to spend money to fix those mistakes. That means she needs more than just a playbook. Your new farmer needs parameters. For example:

- "The monthly budget for facility repairs is $200. You don't need my permission to spend it."
- "This is a Walmart gift card with a $500 balance. Use it for cleaning supplies as needed. Let me know when it runs low."
- "The bookkeeper has been told to designate two hours per week to track our metrics. Please make sure you give her what she needs every Friday. But please hold her to two hours."

The farmer might be called a general manager (or even a COO), but the level of responsibility they acquire when the tinker leaves can't be overlooked.

THE TINKER'S ROLE PROGRESSION

More than once, I've tried to abdicate my way out of a company far too soon. Lousy delegation in my gym cost me over $6,000 in recurring revenue in the past. A lousy partnership choice almost cost me another local company. In both cases, I was sucked back into the day-to-day operations to stop the nosedive, and that pulled me away from the better opportunity. If you're in the Tinker phase, who's your farmer?

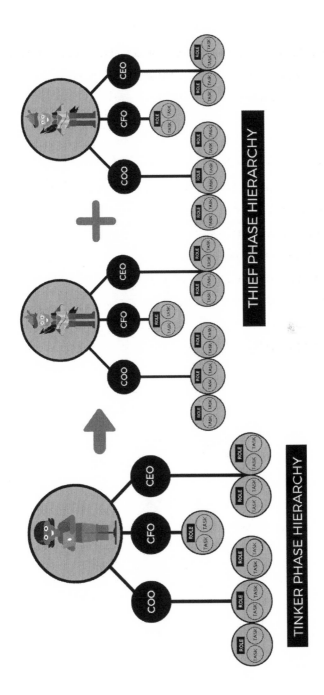

THIEF PHASE HIERARCHY

TINKER PHASE HIERARCHY

"I'm ready to work on the next project, so I took a business partner to keep my business running. But he's dropping the ball, and I'm constantly being called in to fight fires!"

Suzanne owns a daycare. It's a great little spot: she has private rooms, a bit of green grass outside, and a waiting list for enrollment. Or, at least, she did.

Last year, Suzanne had a great idea: to open a kids' used clothing store. As a parent, she knew how quickly kids outgrew expensive sweaters and jeans. And as a daycare owner, she already had a huge mailing list for potential clients. Everything about the idea was solid, so she leased a storefront downtown and opened up.

Knowing that her daycare business was indeed the "golden goose," Suzanne was worried that it would falter without her constant presence. Her idea was to give the daycare manager, Mike, a share of the business. Mike would have some "skin in the game," some upside to growth, and an incentive to work hard. After all, no one works harder than an owner—or so Suzanne thought.

The first week, Mike wanted to repaint one of the kids' rooms. Suzanne had chosen blue for a reason—it's calming for little kids—but she wanted Mike to feel like a real owner, so she let him make his first decision. After all, micromanaging him would defeat the purpose. Right?

Over the next few months, Mike's attitude toward the daycare began to cool. He started wearing jeans and a T-shirt to work, started showing up late, and began yelling at staff. He adopted the privileges of ownership but seemed to avoid the mantle of responsibility.

More and more frequently, Suzanne received texts from other staff, calls from parents, and emails from creditors. She had to rush to the daycare to open the door for the team because Mike was late without warning. She could feel herself getting sucked back in. Worst of all, enrollment was declining, and Suzanne was afraid she'd have to chip in some money to cover payroll. She called me because she was dreading the conversation with Mike. As a shareholder, he'd have to put some money into the business, and Suzanne didn't think he could afford it.

Here are Suzanne's real problems:

- She didn't clearly lay out the potential downside to Mike. She merely handed him a winning lottery ticket.
- She didn't consider other options instead of giving up shares (revenue splits, bonuses, salaries).
- She didn't test her processes to see if her daycare really COULD run without her.

- She didn't test Mike's leadership skills.
- She tried to abdicate instead of delegate.
- She didn't ask Mike if he wanted to be an entrepreneur.

In the words of Jay Williams, a senior Two-Brain Business mentor: "Everyone thinks they want our job. But nobody *really* wants our job." The lure of entrepreneurship is sexy, and staff often only see the upside—time, freedom, and extra money—but no one hears about failing businesses because the entrepreneurs don't talk about them.

Suzanne's first step was to ask the question she should have asked first: "Mike, do you want to own part of this business?" Was it too late to ask? Maybe, but it would let Suzanne give Mike an opportunity to bow out gracefully, save herself a tough conversation, and allow him to escape the cash call. Even if there was a 10 percent chance Mike would say, "Yes, I want to go back to being an employee!" it was worth asking the question.

Next, Suzanne needed to explain the crisis without pointing fingers or laying blame, advise Mike of the future cash call, and ask him if he could make his contribution. From there, the conversation would likely take one of three paths:

1. Mike could say, "Yes, I'll pay," and they could begin dissecting the problem.
2. He could say, "I don't have the money!" and Suzanne could offer to cover the cash crisis in return for his shares.
3. He could respond with, "What the hell happened? This can't be true!" and try to derail the conversation.

Of all the options, Suzanne felt number two was the most likely—Mike was unlikely to doubt her motives, and the bank balance supported her case—and she was right. The crisis proved to be a huge opportunity for Suzanne to regain control over her company...and for Mike to get what HE wanted, which was a secure job.

Though Mike loved to say, "I'm an owner," he didn't really want the responsibilities of ownership. He felt as if Suzanne had "abandoned" him to the business and was unreachable. Suzanne admitted that she had been focusing all of her attention on the clothing store, believing the daycare was in good hands. If not for the cash crisis, Mike and Suzanne might have been able to work through their problems as partners. But ultimately, Mike didn't have the money to cover the costs and had to sell his share of the company back to Suzanne.

It was a costly lesson for her. First, the business should never have reached the cash crisis point. And second, though Mike sold his shares and is back to employee status, he's suspicious of Suzanne and probably looking for a job elsewhere.

Suzanne said, "I wish I'd just paid him to be a manager, or at least tried to explain the downside of ownership before I gave him a share of my baby."

I don't often hear "My business is a cash machine," but I love it when I do! I get excited for the entrepreneur because I know they have another big idea in mind and it's incredibly exciting. The next trick is to keep the first business thriving while the entrepreneur shifts focus to new opportunities. It may mean leaving a farmer behind and, sometimes, taking a partner. But before you take a partner, make sure they REALLY want to be an entrepreneur!

THE TINKER'S MENTOR

Mentorship in the Tinker phase includes two facets: the focused guidance of one objective expert and the support of peers at your level or above.

Every entrepreneur has many great ideas, so a mentor must help them set a time line and keep them focused on two to three projects or objectives. A mentor's other task is to help the tinker set aggressive goals and work toward achieving them. This means a careful codification of the target, a thorough examination of the tinker's reasons for choosing that goal, and then accountability on the steps necessary to achieve it.

Peer support pushes the tinker while the mentor pulls them. At this stage, first-time tinkers might not believe their giant goal is possible or have persistent doubts about their ability to attain them. Peers at the same level can be a tremendous source of encouragement and support. You are the average of the five people you spend the most time with.

This push-pull combo of mentorship and peer support goes way beyond focus and cheerleading. Here are just some of the essential benefits I get from mine.

A paring-down. I speak to my mentor once a month and usually start my calls with a list of huge new ideas. By the end of the call, I have three action items to work toward, and everything else is on hold. That means I actually accomplish three things instead of starting twelve.

Accountability. He emails me every month to ask if I'm on track to hit my goals. As an entrepreneur, my goals are never far from my mind, but these questions force me to objectively assess my progress. When I'm off track, it's always because I tried to start something new instead of working hard on the REAL stuff.

Reassurance and inspiration. There will always be a "dark night of the soul"—sometimes once per month—when a tough problem keeps you awake and stressed. You don't need a solution on those nights but reassurance. I have a picture on my phone of my skis sitting empty on a trail. I was miles away from home, skiing in a forest, when I called my mentor for help on a problem that exercise wasn't solving for me. I paced around a tree while he talked me through it. And the funny part: I already knew the right answer. He just pared away all the wrong answers.

A community of support. On the first weekend with my current mentoring group, I was intimidated. Everyone except me earned between $2 million and $5 million per year, and they were all much heavier hitters than I. But the first topic that came up at a social was the "impostor syndrome," and one brave soul shared that he didn't feel worthy of his success and wasn't sure he could lead his company to the next level.

The next morning, I led the group through a short workout, and another heavy hitter confided that she was nervous about working out. I got to feel useful, and then I got to feel like I was part of it.

Objectivity. It's very easy to talk ourselves into, well, *anything*. Entrepreneurs are exceptional at convincing themselves that their newest idea is their best idea. We fall in love with novelty and chase shiny objects. We need someone to call us on our own BS.

Skin in the game. There are plenty of volunteer organizations that will give you advice. Some of this advice is good, but if you're not paying for it—or if you're not paying an uncomfortable price—you won't act on it. This is true of cheap gym memberships, free lemonade, and free advice.

I'm in a position of privilege. I get to mentor entrepreneurs around the world in a variety of businesses. If there's a mentor in your field, find them. If they've mentored others, even better. (As every athlete knows, top performers don't always make the best coaches.) But even the worst coach is better than no coach. Find a mentor before you take another step. Then find a peer group. Don't try to traverse the Tinker stage alone.

CASE STUDY: THE LONE WOLF

"I don't have anyone to talk to."

I had flown out to Montana to meet with Matt, a CEO who built a very successful company with around one hundred staff in the US and another one hundred in Europe. We spent the first day surrounded by his team and touring the company's different departments. As soon as his last employee left the room, however, those were the first words out of his mouth.

It was probably an entrepreneur who coined "It's lonely at the top." In the Founder phase, the majority of business owners are operating solo. As the business grows, the owner employs staff and becomes surrounded by people. Even into the Tinker phase, when the owner interacts only with high-level staffers, he's still not communicating with other owners.

Matt couldn't share the business's struggles with his staff because they rarely have context. He couldn't vent about the night of lost sleep over a cash flow crisis with his employees because they'd panic and start polishing their résumés. And a month with record-breaking profit also couldn't be shared because his staff would ask for raises that normal cash flow couldn't support.

But Matt didn't want to spend family time talking about the business either. He wanted to be present for his kids, fully immersed in what *they* wanted to talk about, and so he bottled up the highs and lows. He told himself that he's the shield between the scary reality of business and their peaceful lives. He martyred himself without complaint... and he had been doing it for years.

Eventually, though, Matt would need a release valve. He

knew that. Many turn to booze. Some turn to worse. And like Matt, they paint it into their self-portrait of martyr-dom: "I'll do whatever it takes to ride this out and protect my family. I won't let this affect them."

Here are Matt's problems:

- No peer support
- No mentor (no sense that "someone else has these problems" or "someone else has already figured this out")
- He only hangs out with his employees
- He's good at delegation, but not great at separating "works with me" from "friend."

Matt wasn't looking for advice. He had a huge business already, and he had a plan for the next few months. What he really needed was support.

First, we found a mentor who had already accomplished one of his goals. I made the introduction for him.

Then we asked the mentor about peer support. Since mentorship is a one-on-one relationship, I thought he needed both. But the peer support didn't have to come from within Matt's industry. It just had to come from people at his level (Tinker phase). I introduced him to our tinker program at Two-Brain Business, and he'll join us in a few months. It's tough to reach Tinker phase, but several others already have, and they'll welcome him.

The bad news: your employees can't relate to your problems. Your family doesn't need to hear about the worldwide shortage of digital paper clips, either. Matt was right about that. But at this level, it's critical to find a mentor who has been there before, and peer support from people who ARE there now.

There's a reason many entrepreneurs call this stage "the Valley of Death." You're way beyond your comfort zone with money. You're hiring people who have more expertise than you. And you're all alone...until you're not. A mentor guides the way, and peer support paves the road.

THE TINKER'S CHALLENGES

You've done it! You're free! You no longer have to open your business at 6 a.m. and spin the "Closed" sign at 9 p.m. You have staff, systems, and automation. You're making enough money to have a comfortable income for your family and a cushion for your business. Things are good. So why can't you stop stressing about your business?

Why do you check the phone fifty times every evening when you should be pushing your kid on a swing set? If your wife has ever called you out (mine certainly has) for checking your phone when you were "off," then you know all too well the challenges facing the tinker.

YOUR BRAIN IS FULL

See that little red dot in the middle of your brain? That's called your amygdala.

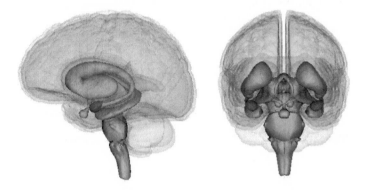

The amygdala's job is fight or flight, baby. It's the GO zone. And everything you encounter—the food you eat, the air you breathe, the people who eyeball you on the subway—they all get processed by the amygdala FIRST. Before you even think about any of that stuff, your amygdala has already made a decision about it. On the plains of Africa, the amygdala learned to trigger the "run away!" response even before your neocortical regions recognized the lion.

Obviously, we aren't on the plains anymore. But as entrepreneurs, we're ALWAYS on the lookout for lions. There are so many ways a business can be killed (especially in the early days) that our amygdala is on constant alert:

- "What's that client going to write about me on Facebook?"
- "How many people are coming through the door today?"
- "Is my assistant's grammar getting better, or do I need to read more of her emails?"
- "Did my lunch make my breath stinky before this meeting?"
- "How am I going to get more clients?"

And your amygdala LIKES it.

This constant vigilance makes your amygdala grow. It recruits other neurons from nearby areas of the brain and says, "I need these more than you do." As it gathers power, your amygdala takes an even bigger role in the brain and evaluates all stimuli for possible threats.

Do entrepreneurs sometimes overreact? Sure we do. And we blame it on fatigue, or stress, or distraction. But it's our amygdala. It's training. It's feeding on our stress and growing. And then, one day, we try to shut it off.

Now, when ordinary people get bored, they tend to create

drama for themselves. A certain amount of positive stress (called "eustress") is natural to keep the amygdala healthy. Think of it as brain exercise: when things are going really well, small problems become big deals. We blow things out of proportion just because we don't have anything else to worry about. We have to fill that amygdala up, and so pebbles become boulders.

When an entrepreneur with his super macho, jacked-up amygdala gets bored, he gets twitchy. His brain needs to be fed, so he goes looking for trouble, problems to solve, or just everyday stimulation: hitting Refresh on email, signing up to test new software, starting fifty new projects. He can't help it because he's wired that way.

How do you rewire yourself to be a normal human again? How do you start to enjoy success, lower your blood pressure, and catch up on the last decade of missed sleep? You have to train your brain.

First, **leave the house**. Get away from screens and phones.

Second, **have predetermined "check-in" times** for email, text, social media, and all other messaging tools.

Third, **exercise**. Rewiring the brain happens much more quickly when you pepper it with BDNF, the chemical you secrete when you exercise. (Dr. John Ratey calls it "Miracle-Gro for the brain.")

Fourth, **go away**. Commit yourself to a family activity that will fully occupy your mind.

Finally, **flush out your brain with writing or other creative tasks,** and finish your day by writing out your bright spots to practice gratitude.

The amygdala is a powerful part of your brain, but it's overridden by the slower neocortex (where you think your thoughts). You can retrain your automatic responses with habits, and override your impulses with logic, but only if you practice.

The brain that got you here won't get you to the next level. So start training your mind—and your body—to be the leader your business needs.

THE MULTITASKING MYTH

Now we're going to play a game. Draw two dots on the floor, about three feet apart. Make each dot just large enough for your feet.

Stand in one circle. Then hop to the other. Make sure both feet land within the circle without touching the edges.

Now jump back. Same rules apply. This is still easy, right? You're not even breaking a sweat yet.

Every two seconds, continue jumping back and forth between the circles. What do you notice? You start to become less accurate. You get tired. You have to try harder to achieve the same result.

Now keep going for eight hours and try to read a book while you're doing it.

This is what happens when we multitask: our brain switches from one circle to the other, becoming less and less efficient. It's called "task switching," a pretty obvious name, and it's really inefficient. Your brain can't hold two projects at the same time; instead, it tries to switch back and forth between the two, like jumping from dot to dot. As your brain fatigues, your cognitive abilities decline. You start missing the mark and then autocorrecting.

The "jumping dots" analogy is a simple one. But what happens in your brain is even worse: as you increase cognitive load over the course of the day, the dots get further and further apart. You have to work harder and harder to get from one thought to another, and you become less and less effective.

The best way to really move the needle in your business is to single-task. How do you do it?

1. Determine when you're naturally most focused. For me, this is four in the morning because no one else is awake and distractions are minimal.
2. Turn off all notifications on your desktop. Move your cell phone at least ten feet away (research shows that a cell phone on your desk consumes mental energy even when it's turned off). Isolate yourself.
3. Do a quick "flow state" focusing exercise.
4. Pick up where you left off: finish a sentence you started yesterday or use another "head start" to get some action going.
5. Make a "later" list where you can quickly cut and paste ideas as they spring to mind. Instead of leaping into the next circle with both feet, write down your idea and return to it the next day. Fear of forgetting is a huge distractor.

Linking several tasks together, one at a time, will get several of them done. Trying to juggle them all at once won't get anything done.

WHAT TO DO WHEN IT ALL GOES WRONG

"We're entrepreneurs. Nobody wants our job, but everybody thinks they do." Those are the wise words of

Two-Brain Business mentor Jay Williams in his speech at one of our summit events. No matter how perfect your preparation or how thorough your practice, things will go wrong in your business. The nature of entrepreneurship is unpredictability, and that rule goes tenfold for the tinker trying to scale his or her business and avoid the Valley of Death. Here's how to manage the stressful times and come out ahead for having them.

Get a mentor. Find somebody else who will say, "I will take partial responsibility for your success. I will answer the phone when you call. I will be available to you. I will share my experience."

Break the problem down into its component parts. Years ago, if a coach had said, "Chris, the members are complaining about the workouts we're giving them," I would have panicked. I would have said, "Oh my God, I have to change something," and I would have immediately thought about how I could do it.

Now I know better. Now I know to break the problem down. My follow-up questions will be, "How many people, what are their names, and what exactly did they say?"

View every new experience as practice. This is called the growth mindset. The growth mindset is basically viewing every new experience as practice, expecting that things won't be perfect the first time, and knowing that it's okay to screw up on this decision because you're going to learn from it. There's a lot of forgiveness that goes into the growth mindset, and the key is to give yourself permission to fail in advance. You are not going to be perfect at this, and that's okay.

I'd like to think that every tough situation that I deal with is preparing me for something even harder ahead. If a staff person quits after they've been with me for ten years, I can say, "Well, this is preparing me for ten years from now when another staff person quits after twenty years." You will learn from these little lessons that seem so big, and you'll be able to avoid the big problems later. The only mistake that's not acceptable is the same mistake made twice.

Remember that business is cyclical. That means there are going to be very high points in your career. You're going to land that deal for $50,000 at that local school. There are also going to be points that are just as low or almost so. What I want you to know is that if you're doing it right and if you're improving your skillset, you'll always trend up.

Pessimism is a habit, so is optimism. Neither of them happens by accident, and both happen because of practice.

I want you to notice how often you're thinking positive thoughts during the day, and how often you're thinking negatively. When I did this exercise, it was 4 a.m., pitch black, I was driving through snow, and I said, "Holy crap. I think days go by when I don't have a single positive thought at all."

What do you think that does to your brain? What do you think all those negative messages are doing to your mind all the time? How might you benefit by practicing more optimism?

Imagine the worst-case scenario. Stoicism is a school of Greek philosophy that's been copied by religions, other philosophies, and "fix-yourself" experts for over four thousand years. Readers of early Stoics, like Epictetus, will find commonalities between Christianity and Buddhism, religions that were formed centuries later.

The philosophy has several central tenets, but this one matters most for me: things could always be worse, which is why you should "practice" for the worst-case scenarios facing your business. As Seneca said: "The man who has anticipated the coming of troubles takes away their power when they arrive."

For example, when a key staff member leaves, it can cause a ton of stress. To overcome the pressure, you have to pick it apart. What's so scary about the staff person leaving? Maybe you're anxious they'll take all of your clients or criticize you in public. So ask yourself, what's the worst-case scenario?

First, will they really take all of your clients or just half of them? What if they *do* take half? Would those clients leave all at once or over the next few months? Which clients would go first? How would they tell you? Put yourself in the frame and really imagine that conversation.

THEN, take action: what can you do TODAY to keep those clients?

Second, if they criticize you in public, what would happen? How would they do it? A post on Facebook? Comments to your colleagues in person? What would they say? What's the worst-case effect it would have?

Then, decide: in the long run, are you better to acknowledge that this might happen and take NO action? Are you better to respond? Can you write blog posts NOW explaining why you do things the way you do? In other words, can you eliminate their criticism by reporting your flaws first?

Considering the worst-case scenario gives you the opportunity to do two things:

- Break the problem down into its component parts without the lens of emotion. This makes the situation solvable.
- Realize that even the WORST case really isn't that bad. In our society, entrepreneurs don't starve.

Dan Martell reinforced this lesson for me when he said, "Problems don't stop, and they don't get smaller." Plan for trouble as readily as you would plan for growth.

Use the challenge as a separator. Before you give up, consider that most of your competitors WILL give up. What if you're the only one who overcomes this obstacle? Will it separate you from them? That's usually enough motivation for me.

Identify what the problems could be in advance. Now, experience, of course, is going to help with this. If you've been through something before, you can share that experience with other people. You can also stop it from happening again next time because you'll recognize the warning signs.

Finding a mentor who has faced the problem already is the best possible investment you can make. You'll leap ahead, usually by years, and save yourself millions of dollars and many sleepless nights by investing in their knowledge.

My last tip is to act with gratitude. How do you practice gratitude? How do you be more than just thankful? The answer is service. Doing things for other people. Not buying stuff for other people, not even writing a thank-you card, but thanking other people, doing a service for them, helping them first—that is what gets you out of stress. The more stressed you are, the more anxiety that you have, the more depression that you find yourself tied up with, the more service you need to do.

When I interviewed Mark Divine, author of *Unbeatable Mind*, he told me, "Every person who can improve themselves and set themselves on a path of self-mastering and service to others will have a ripple effect across the world. That's my main thing is to send ripples across the world to try to improve individuals who then will improve their families, and then they will improve their communities, improve their countries, and then improve the world at large."

Remember, you're doing this because you want to, not because you have to. You always have choices, and the biggest decision you have in life is how you respond to things that stress you out. I said "respond" because I don't mean react. I mean plan for it. Train yourself to respond to stress with patience, self-forgiveness, and gratitude.

CASE STUDY: THE IMPOSTOR

"Who am I to lead this massive company?"

Casey's company has grown tremendously in the years I've known him. When I met him, Casey was running a small personal training business in Maine. He was coaching most of the clients himself, keeping his appointments on a scribble pad, and tracking his expenses in his head. He was paying himself but had no idea how to stop working a seventy-hour week or earn more money or hire another coach.

Now he does.

Still it didn't surprise me when Casey reached out with a story.

"I was just in the shower," it began. "I dropped my razor. It's one of those with the interchangeable heads. The head broke off. I couldn't figure out how to get it back on again. First, I got pissed because I thought 'everyone else knows how to do this. The commercials make it look easy.' And then my mind jumped to 'Who the hell am I to lead a million-dollar company? I can't even fix my cheap plastic razor!'"

Casey has impostor syndrome, and it's not rare. At some point, most successful entrepreneurs have the fleeting thought that they've woken up in someone else's life and aren't equipped to handle it. Though they can remember every excruciating detail of their climb up the ladder, they feel they've somehow failed to acquire the skills necessary to exist at the top.

Here are Casey's real problems:

1. He needs higher-level financial reporting so he can see trends instead of just checking his daily bank balance. He also needs some forecasting, a safety net, and a plan for the future.
2. He needs someone else to manage day-to-day operations so he can focus on growth.
3. He needs a strategy for growing his business.
4. He needs a plan for growing himself as a leader.

For the first time, Casey is hiring people with more specialized knowledge than he has. He's making financial commitments at a level he's never made before. He's removing himself from daily operations. And—more than ever—he feels totally alone.

My first strategy with Casey was to identify three meta roles in his business: a CFO, a COO, and a CSO. "Now pick one," I said, "and replace yourself in the other two."

This is an expensive process but a necessary one. Casey's

business is just too big for him to try to be an expert at everything. He could choose to become an expert at sales and marketing, or he could become an accountant, or he could manage the delivery of his product. He chose the latter.

First, we found Casey an external CFO. The new chair worked remotely and produced some new reports that would allow Casey to track where his money comes from, where he's missing opportunities, and where his money goes. She'll help him decide whether to buy a new building or open another location or to invest in market funds or other businesses.

Second, we discussed hiring an ad agency for marketing but decided to optimize his sales and conversion process first. Casey has a lot of leads on his email list, so we began training someone else to approach them. If that person works out, we'll teach them to run ad campaigns through the Two-Brain Business marketing program.

Third—and this was the fun part for Casey—we started an operations improvement plan. Casey signed up for a course on corporate culture-building and booked a visit at another gym with a larger team.

MOST importantly, Casey joined a mastermind group of other tinkers for peer support. It really is lonely at the top of his little mountain. He needs to hear that others are going through the same challenges.

Casey still has a way to go before he can retire. He'll gradually upgrade his leadership skills, reinforce the mission of his team, and spread his influence. But that hard work will create a platform on which Casey can build a legacy. With a broad revenue base, increasing time and devotion to service, Casey can leverage the hard lessons of the Tinker phase to make a real difference in the world.

For many entrepreneurs, the Tinker phase is the end goal. But for those seeking to really make a mark, the Thief phase beckons.

ARE YOU READY TO BE A THIEF?

Have you hired three meta roles (COO, CFO, CSO)?

Have you tested abdication of your primary business?

Have you set up at least three paths to passive income for retirement?

Have you hired a mentor?

Have you begun measuring and training for flow-state time?

Have you written an annual plan for scaling, diversifying, or starting your next business?

Have you built or joined a group of peers, like a mastermind?

Have you built your tax strategy?

Have you chosen your retirement date?

Is your EHR over $500 per hour?

Have you begun mentoring your staff or others in your industry?

Are you exercising at least four times per week with appropriate intensity?

PART FOUR

—

THIEF

"Don't find customers for your products, find products for your customers."

—SETH GODIN

You've made it. You can stop now. But why would you want to? After sowing the seeds, tilling the soil, and finally reaping the harvest, what comes next?

On my introductory visit with my first mentor, he asked me, "What scares you most about business?"

I thought for a moment (I had many fears) and answered, "That I'll never be able to retire from this."

He nodded and said, "You're never going to retire, anyway. Stop worrying about it."

I didn't stop worrying, but I started to see retirement differently.

For our parents, "retirement" meant golf and game shows on television. It meant an end. To us, retirement means *choice*. We can choose how we spend our time and money. We can choose when to work and how much. But most entrepreneurs will never be done. When the fields have been harvested, it's time to sow seeds again.

Of course, after scrambling through the Founder stage, working through the Farmer stage and surviving the Tinker stage, few entrepreneurs want to start from scratch. To those who do, I salute you. The second time should be more straightforward and faster than the first.

The opportunities available to a thief are of a higher order. A founder links her idea to her labor. A farmer links his idea to profit. A tinker links her idea to her lifestyle. A thief links his idea to other ideas and creates opportunities for others while doing so. The thief has a bank of experience, a bank of knowledge, and a bank of money.

And the smart thief will take a much easier, faster route:

1. They'll find a new niche for their service.
2. They'll find a partner to upgrade their distribution model.

3. They'll make small, regular upgrades to their service.
4. Or they'll sell.

The best thieves are often those who fought hard through the founder and Farmer phases. They have the most to contribute. They're the best teachers and mentors and coaches because they've done it themselves, and now they're ready to leverage that pain to move mountains for others.

THE NOBLE THIEF

"He stole from the rich and gave to the poor" goes the story of Robin Hood, the medieval archer, and his band of merry men. Now, to be clear, the Thief stage isn't about breaking the law, and it is NOT about ripping off another founder's ideas. There's a vast difference between stealing another entrepreneur's idea for your own use and partnering with him for the better good of all. I use the Robin Hood story to illustrate our noble intentions here. The best entrepreneurs understand that they'll make more money growing the pie than trying to cut a larger slice.

The noble thief moves resources from an area of high concentration to low concentration and, like Robin Hood, builds a legacy of service to his community. Your goal in this phase is to find those you can partner with to bring your idea to a new audience or combine your ideas to creating even bigger ones. It's also to create a legacy of service within your community through volunteerism, philanthropy, endowment, or mentorship. Success in the Thief phase means building a platform that continues your service after you're gone.

As a founder, I struck out on my own, opened a gym, and trained every client personally. In the Farmer phase, I spent over a decade making my business self-sustaining. As a tinker, I opened several other companies and began mentoring other entrepreneurs. Now, as a thief, I plan to gather my band of merry men and move wealth to the most deserving: other entrepreneurs who take risks to change lives. My mission is to guide 1,000,000 entrepreneurs to wealth.

Building something bigger than your business is essential at this stage. I know that because I'm in it too. As a thief, my goal is now to expand my mission and transition Two-Brain Business into other industries. By bringing these strategies to other businesses, such as dental offices, I can help improve the companies in my community and leave a lasting impact—one that will survive long after I'm gone.

The Thief stage differs immensely from the founder, farmer, and Tinker stages, and so the sections to come will be different too, less tactical and more inspirational.

The noble thief's story transcends generations and inspires others.

What's next for you?

How will your kids remember you?

How will your team remember you?

How will your community remember you?

THE THIEF'S KEYWORD: WEALTH

There's a classic story about a businessman and a fisherman in which the vacationing businessman hires the fisherman to take him out on the water for the day. They have a lot of fun, catch a few fish, share some stories, and at the end of the day, the businessman hands the fisherman some money and asks, "So what are you going to do next?"

The fisherman says, "I'll go and take a nap. Then I'll meet my friends at a little bar. We'll drink wine, and I'll play the guitar, and we'll all sing songs. I'll go home, make love to my wife, and sleep in tomorrow. Then I might get a late breakfast and go fishing awhile."

"You know, you could charge a lot more than you do," the

businessman replies. "Guys like me could pay twice as much."

The fisherman shrugs and asks, "What would I do with the money?"

The businessman says, "Well, you could buy a nicer, bigger boat."

"And then what?"

The businessman thinks for a moment and answers, "Well, you could take twice as many people at a time. You could make even more money and hire someone to help you."

The fisherman nods and says, "That sounds pretty good. Then what?"

"Well, eventually, you could own two boats—maybe a whole fleet! You'd hire captains to run the boats for you and make a killing!"

"That sounds great! Then what?"

"Well, you'd try to sell off the big company or open franchises in other destinations. You'd be rich!"

"Wow," says the fisherman. "What would I do then?"

To which the businessman acknowledges, "Well, you could retire to a little beach somewhere, drink wine and play your guitar all night, sleep late, and maybe do a little fishing."

It's a quaint story, and I think of it every time I catch myself putting the pursuit of money ahead of something more important, like my family or my perfect day. This tale of the businessman and the fisherman reminds me that wealth takes different shapes. Material ownership is a part of it, of course, but real wealth is *freedom*:

- **Freedom of time:** The ability to choose how you invest your day.
- **Freedom of experience:** The opportunity to immerse yourself in new places, new cultures, and new adventures.
- **Freedom of finances:** Self-reliance, security, and the knowledge that you'll sleep in a warm bed with a full belly—and the confidence that your position won't change tomorrow.
- **Freedom of choice:** Independence, agency, and the power to decide your own path.
- **Freedom of pursuit:** The opportunity to dedicate yourself to fulfilling your real potential.

- **Freedom of generosity:** The chance to share and lift others up.
- **Freedom of mindset:** Abundance, patience, peace. Escape from a mentality of competition, jealousy, and comparison.
- **Freedom of commitment:** The ability to commit time and resources for as long as necessary.
- **Freedom of legacy:** The opportunity to leave a multigenerational platform of service or support, to write your own story, and to impact the minds of future generations.
- **Freedom of health:** Controlling your own mobility. Freedom from the bonds of medication, weakness, or mental decline.

The fisherman in our story had elements of wealth. Though cash poor, he had the freedom of time and chose where to allocate his hours every day. He could spend time with his wife and community every evening, which allowed him to feel important as a husband and friend. He had his health, access to clean air, and lots of sunlight. And he spent his days doing what most of us would consider a vacation. In fact, money might be the only element of wealth he lacked. So why didn't the businessman consider him wealthy?

The answer, of course, is capital. Money is the great enabler, and most of the other facets of wealth require it. Money creates time, funds a business's growth and expansion, and money serves...but money alone isn't wealth. It's just one shape wealth takes. *Real wealth* is our aim in the Thief phase.

THE THIEF'S #HASHTAG

The hashtags that describe a thief might be #legacy or #connection, and this stage presents the opportunity and the responsibility for both. As a thief, your opportunities for connection expand on horizontal and vertical planes. Horizontal connections are opportunities. You can expand your big idea, or business, into parallel industries. Vertical connections are responsibilities. You can mentor others in your niche to build a legacy or receive mentorship from those who have come before you. Ideally, you'll do both.

First, the horizontal connections: a thief must use her time to find niches in which she can duplicate her idea. Ask, "Where else would this idea apply? Who else can I serve through duplication of my primary service?"

For example, I initially built the Two-Brain Incubator for gym owners. But many gym owners have partners or investors who own other businesses. As we heard feedback like, "Hey, I used this in my law practice, and it worked great!" and "This would apply so well to my bakery!" we knew we could help people in those niches. And so TwoBrain.com was born, with a perfect Incubator program for any service-based business. I have already tested the lessons and tactics and one-on-one mentorship with over five hundred entrepreneurs. Nothing like it exists anywhere else. It's a win for entrepreneurs everywhere, a win for our mentors, and a win for Two-Brain Business.

One of our clients did the same in reverse. He built billing software for law practices. When it proved lucrative, he invested in a gym and used the same software there. Now it's gaining popularity in the second niche.

Another client built a retail solution for gym owners. Instead of wasting time designing T-shirts, owners could choose from a variety of templates, upload their logo, and have their design tweaked by a professional. They could then have their clients preorder gym-branded clothing and never spend a cent on extra inventory. It was a huge win for gym owners, who rarely have the extra capital to tie up in shelf stock. When the program garnered a lot of success, the shirt company asked themselves, "Who else has this same problem?" and found other niches to serve. That's #connection: moving across the landscape to find similar niches.

However, the founders of those companies can also

help others within their original niche. These are vertical connections. They can mentor other founders. They can employ other founders or even acquire companies whose services complement their own. This is #legacy: empowering others to build on your original brand or idea. Entrepreneurship can echo forever through mentorship.

THE THIEF'S VALUES

The thief supports the community's values where they intersect with her own. If you care about yourself, then you have to care about the community around you, and if you care about them, then you have to care about their environment: what they eat, what they do, what they breathe. The thief looks for opportunities to contribute to their communities.

First, **your business community**:

- What is important to your clients?
- What do they want NOW?

As your influence grows, you will have the power to help more people. But what kinds of help do they need? How will your help fit into their lives? What are their values?

In my case, my business community was other gym owners. Here's what was important to them:

- **Transparency.** They wanted to hear about what I had done, not what I would do.
- **Authenticity.** They wanted me to remain a gym owner, like them.
- **Humility.** Plenty of "experts" in our niche know everything and never, ever make mistakes. I'm not one of them.

As my gym righted itself, I shared my mistakes and the lessons I learned the hard way with other owners. I was authentic, humble, transparent to the point of TMI, and I genuinely cared about them and wanted to help them succeed. I found the intersection of my values and theirs—helping people—and unlocked my new direction: I would help gym owners grow their businesses to help hundreds of other people. I would become a better business coach than a fitness coach.

Second, **your life community:**

- What do your family and friends NEED?
- How can you help?
- How might that become a legacy project?
- How do you set your kids up for success?

Your answers will depend on your values. When it comes to your community of family and friends, make your own rules. That's your privilege. I use the $10,000 rule. Find a place where your money will have an immediate and profound impact. It's an approach I picked up from Greg Glassman.

"Find places where $10,000 will make an immediate and profound difference." That was Greg's advice to me in 2015. He had recently spent millions of his own dollars supporting some big charities and using his CrossFit community to raise millions more, and we were talking about what he'd learned from it. It's easy to throw money into a big fundraising machine, and heaven knows they exist for a reason, but my favorite story about Greg's altruism isn't the millions raised for cancer research or the schools built in Kenya. It's this one.

When Greg was visiting a US city on one of his cross-country gym tours, he met a woman who was cleaning her local gym in exchange for her membership. She couldn't afford to pay the monthly fee because her son required round-the-clock care at home. She left the house only twice a day: to exercise and to clean the gym. As they talked, the woman confessed that her son had to sleep in a bathtub because his physical challenges required a special bed she couldn't afford.

Greg at once bought the boy a new bed...AND a special chair and a new tub. Ten thousand dollars changed that woman's family's life forever.

You won't find this story printed in glossy profiles. Greg didn't even tell me this story himself. It came to me the way all stories about great givers do, through a third party, and several others have confirmed it. I know it happened because I know Greg's values. He follows the $10,000 rule, and so do I. Where in your community will $10,000 (or $1,000) make a measurable and life-changing difference?

A thief's wealth isn't limited to money; neither should his contribution be. Often, the time you contribute is worth far more than any check you'll sign.

Early in my career, I had a client named Paul. Paul was an entrepreneur who employed several staff members. He and his wife were amazing parents to their own kids and also volunteered as foster parents to many others.

Paul and I were talking about his contribution to our community one day. I told him that his ability to foster the kids inspired me, but I couldn't follow his example. I thought sending the kids back to poverty—sometimes abuse—after getting to know them would be way too hard on me.

"How do you DO it?" I asked. "How can you go through the torment, again and again, of becoming attached to these kids, knowing they'll spend most of their lives without the love and support you're giving them?"

I've never forgotten Paul's answer.

"If all you get them for is a few days," he said, "then you just hope those few days are enough."

I'm sure Paul's caring home showed many local kids that things could be different for them. And I'm sure many followed his example instead of repeating the cycle of victimhood. Paul inspired me to share where I could. Where will one hundred hours of your time change the course of a life?

Finally, consider **your community at large**:

- What can you share?
- Where can you collaborate to contribute more?
- You may find it easy to identify a need in your city, but where can your expertise help most?

My kids' passions drew us to hockey sponsorship. We live in a rural community, and many parents don't have the time or money required to keep their kids in sports. When support dried up for a local team, my wife and I saw a golden opportunity and swooped in to pay for jerseys, equipment, and travel. I remember the joyful rush to beat everyone else to the hotel so we could secretly pay for several rooms without the families finding out who the "sponsor" was.

But as time went on, the team's real needs emerged: the kids needed coaching. I was never a high-level hockey player myself but had already spent over twenty years coaching kids. I felt I could contribute, and when the opportunity arose, I had the time to step in and donate my time and attention. When I was still in the founder or Farmer phases, I didn't have the time or mental bandwidth to share. Now, as a thief, I can.

The other great need in my community—and probably in yours—is entrepreneurial support.

I spent the first ten years of entrepreneurship listening to my clients tell me that our city was doomed, that the failing steel mill would mean the end of all local business. I didn't listen because I couldn't give in to that fear: if my company failed, my family would go hungry. I had to learn how to identify my best clients and focus on them, I had to learn how to sell and market better, and I had to learn how to keep clients for a long time.

The steel mill DID fail, and so did the paper mill—the city's two largest employers—but it happened gradually. I protected my gym by tightening up our processes and diversifying our revenue streams, and we weren't affected. Unfortunately, not every business in the city prepared the way I did or had the entrepreneurial mentorship I received during this tough time. Some went under.

My community of business owners needed the resources and expertise I could give them.

My mission became obvious: to start a local center for entrepreneurship, to support local entrepreneurs through seminars and mentorship, and to help guide our economy back to prosperity, just as my first mentor, Denis, had done for me.

I was part of his legacy, and through Two-Brain Business I now have the platform to help dozens of other local entrepreneurs.

THE THIEF'S KINGMAKER EQUATION

Wealth has two sides: money and time. Money can be spent, but so can time. So can energy. So can care. And your wealth investment strategy is only half complete if it doesn't factor in how your time gets invested. In the Thief phase, your goal is to reach an EHR of over $5,000. The best way to do that is to make others wealthy while you free up your time. I recommend carving out a minimum of three hours.

If you need a template, start with these three hours:

- Spend one hour every day as a CEO, not a coach or bookkeeper or Facebook reader.

- Dedicate one hour per day to an idea. Nurture connections that will grow your platform. Make decisions, seek new opportunities, or just spend time thinking.
- Spend one hour working on YOU. Do physical workouts, study leadership, go to counseling sessions. Enter the flow state. At the end of each day, ask yourself, "Am I a better person now than I was at breakfast?"

Wealth produces a broad and stable platform. When your basic health, security, and social needs are met, you're free to work on societal problems. You can dedicate your time to service. You can pursue self-actualization by giving to others: your capital resources, your time, and your knowledge. True wealth, as we've discussed, extends far beyond capital.

THE THIEF'S INCOME GOAL

In many ways, the Thief stage is about reaping the proverbial harvest, but you must always save a part of the crop for replanting. That means reinvestment: financial, emotional, and familial. Your "seeds" might change too. I made my first money selling fitness, but my new investments are all made to help others sell fitness:

- I invest money in technology that will help gyms.
- I invest time in local entrepreneurs who can change our city.

- I invest care in local kids who need some "bright spots."

As a thief, your income goal is straightforward: earn enough to last you to age 150, possibly enough to have a multigenerational impact.

First, your investments must create a return that allows you to live on the income. This could be the interest on your investments, the rent on your buildings, or a dividend on your corporate shares. It could be fees paid to you from companies you own or advise. But the income must NOT require you to attend a set schedule. You're no longer paid to show up.

If large enough, your investments can also pay others. I like to work backward from the legacy I want to create. A scholarship fund, for example, might take as little as $5,000 to start, or you might prefer to create a fund with $200,000 that will generate enough interest to offer scholarships every year in perpetuity. There are even simpler ways to approach your investing too.

Every Sunday morning, I take an hour to work out in my garage, and I often listen to Jim Rohn while I work on cleans, jerks, and then snatches. Rohn is old school, and he proposes a 70-10-10-10 split for your income. He teaches this split to entrepreneurs and kids, and if you don't have a better plan, it's a great starting point. Here's how Rohn splits a dollar:

- First, put a dime toward charity or worthy causes.
- Next, take a dime to invest in yourself.
- Finally, invest a dime in something that will work on your behalf.
- Spend the other 70 cents supporting yourself and your family.

The ten cents to charity is self-explanatory. Whether you frequent a church and commit to tithing or write a monthly check to a good cause, that dime is well spent.

The second dime is to use on asset creation. Invest in your business, buy a building, start a new company, or pay for training. This investment should yield an increase in wealth: more money, less time.

The third is for investing in someone else's idea or company. Put it into a 401k, the stock market, or shares in other companies. While I'm not qualified to advise anyone else, I keep these investments on the conservative side, like index funds. Though I get better at entrepreneurialism every day and have learned to mitigate risk, owning one business IS riskier than owning 500. Index funds, the average of hundreds of companies, are my "hedge."

The real earnings goal in the Thief phase is to control where your earnings go. If you'd prefer they go to your children instead of the tax office, take steps long before your demise to avoid putting that inheritance at risk. At this stage, you might also consider your time as your most important investment.

THE THIEF'S TIME GOAL

After leading an employee buyout at a massive lumber mill, Denis was recruited to become CEO of our local steel mill. In his first year, he accepted company stock for payment instead of a salary. The company was trading for under a dollar at the time (seventy cents per share rings a bell). A few years later, Denis sold his shares at their new value—over $50 each—and retired.

He decided his legacy would be to serve as a mentor to five local business owners. I was one of them, and I was in trouble.

A month earlier, I found myself on a park bench asking myself, "Am I ever going to succeed at this?" I'd been struggling in the Founder phase for years. I had just missed our second consecutive paycheck and barked at my wife for buying "the expensive cheese." It was finally clear. I wasn't going to just "figure it out" or grind my way to success.

Luckily, one of the city's business planning officers used to play football. I trained him as a teenager, and we stayed friends through his college career. When the opportunity to work with Denis came up, Mike immediately filled out the application for me.

I'm not sure how he determined his rates, but the check I wrote to Denis on the first day seemed astronomical, and to be honest, it should have bounced. But I think Denis knew I had to be a little scared because there was hard work ahead. The price was painful on purpose. He knew he needed to hold my attention.

So what did Denis charge for his mentorship? $500. His time was worth about ten times that amount, and the value his mentorship provided me was priceless. Denis's impact has already had a multigenerational legacy in my family. My kids are interested in entrepreneurship. My ten-year-old is telling me about his comic book business as I write this section, and my daughter started selling books online when she was eight. It was the best $500 I've ever spent.

After mentoring over 500 entrepreneurs from all corners of the earth, I now understand why Denis did it. He saw his time as a gift he could give. The time goal of the thief is to give gifts of time.

As much as I'd like to donate a billion dollars to charity or create an endowment fund, my real mission is to create a multigenerational impact. I want to empower others to create wealth for themselves, success for their staff, and growth for their communities, and like Denis, I can do that by giving my time.

Entrepreneurs play a foundational role in their communities. They're also excellent leverage points. When an entrepreneur succeeds, he pulls his family, his staff, their families, and his customers up with him. He spends his money locally, paying taxes and eating at restaurants. Those people benefit too. One small step for entrepreneurship can build a larger platform for an entire town. And I can help them take that small step.

Only after failing, only after struggling, only after openly sharing my challenging times am I now in the position to help others. My first book was just a collection of blog posts. It didn't have page numbers, let alone a professional editor. And it sold 20,000 copies because it was authentic. It gave me the platform to guide other gym owners toward profitability. And as they told their friends about Two-Brain Business, other service providers began to ask for help.

As a thief, my mission is to help 1,000,000 entrepreneurs become wealthy. Two-Brain Business is my platform for mentorship. Programs like the Incubator take founders to the Farmer phase, and programs like Authority Ladder help other entrepreneurs spread their message around the world. A rising tide (and gifted time) lifts all boats.

THE THIEF'S BRAND

In the Thief phase, your business should operate autonomously. The first sign that I'd solved my "icon problem" happened at 12:03 p.m. on a Monday. I had been traveling the week earlier and arrived late to my CrossFit class. When I burst through the door, the rest of the group was following the coach through a warm-up.

The closest person to me in the group was a face I didn't recognize. She stuck out her hand, and said, "Hi, you must be new here! I'm Sarah."

My wife was stretching nearby and cracked up when she overheard Sarah's introduction. I beamed. I'd long ago lost the ego around owning a gym in favor of owning a company that ran without me.

It's common for a thief to become a brand unto himself or herself. In the same way that LeBron James transcends the Cavaliers, Heat, or Lakers, an entrepreneur's fame can eventually transcend their business. Elon Musk is a great example. His personal brand is so powerful that he can now raise funds for new companies based on his previous success. Other entrepreneurs compete for his attention and partnership. This personal brand is best described as your authority. Your ability to serve expands with your platform of wealth. The broader your influence, the more people you can serve. The deeper they trust you, the better you can serve them.

BUILDING YOUR BRAND BEYOND YOU

A founder asks, "How will this help me?" A farmer asks, "How will this help my staff?" A tinker asks, "How will this help my community?" The thief is the connector of ideas. He asks, "How will this help everyone?"

Often a thief will identify an opportunity outside his original niche where his service can fit with a few alterations. For example, a software developer might discover that his booking and billing app for dentists is also a perfect fit for medical doctors. He'll partner with an authority in the space, make a few changes, and leverage his partner's authority to introduce his service to a new niche.

Entrepreneurs in the Thief phase cultivate these relationships by seeking out other thieves, attending entrepreneurial meet-ups or summit events, and reading across a broad spectrum. A good thief is curious and seeks opportunities in unfamiliar territory. Many in the Thief phase travel and bring new ideas back to their turf.

Another example might be a restaurateur who visits Malaysia on a visit. While spending a month relaxing, she samples local cooking styles and realizes that some dishes would complement the food she serves in her restaurant. She brings techniques and recipes home and creates new dishes that are even better than the originals. The borrowed ideas are more than the sum of their parts. She creates a new category through the fusion of two cultural styles.

It's important for those in the Thief phase to prioritize experiences over the mere accumulation of money. Our growth toward self-actualization depends on the depth of our experience. And our pursuit of wealth depends on broadening our horizons.

One of the greatest connections I've made happened between two unrelated industries: real estate and the fitness business. As a young entrepreneur, I was given a copy of *Rich Dad, Poor Dad* by Robert Kiyosaki. I fell in love with his "buy and hold" ideology from the very first page. Everyone around me was talking about buying stocks for their retirement—this was before the crash of 2008—but Kiyosaki introduced me to the accumulation of cash flow assets.

Kiyosaki's strategy is to buy rental properties with the bank's money and keep them forever, collecting rent above the mortgage cost. For example, he would buy a building with a $500 monthly mortgage payment and then rent the building for $550 per month. He'd make a small profit up front, and a larger profit when the mortgage ended. But the key is that he doesn't put his own money at risk, and the income is passive. He doesn't have to punch a clock or take any action beyond the initial purchase.

I immediately saw the implications for a commercial rental property: multiple tenants paying rent, shorter repayment periods, and a longer rental period after the mortgage. I had already planned to purchase a building for my gym, but I wondered, "Can this be done with a business?" Would it be possible to build a business that's hands-off and allow it to generate revenue even when I wasn't there? Could I, in effect, retire from my business but still make a paycheck?

It took me nearly a decade, but I did it. My business—heavy on personal service with its clients—runs autonomously. I own the building in which the gym sits. The gym pays me rent, plus a wage above the average family income in our city. In 2018, I set a goal to stay out of the gym for six straight months. I didn't tell my staff. I told my friends I was training for a bike race instead... And I did it. I didn't miss a single paycheck, and I didn't set foot in my gym for six straight months.

If I sold Catalyst six months ago, I might have earned $500,000 on the sale. (I won't get into the math here or why I didn't sell it for more.) But let's say I sold it for a million dollars, which would be astronomical for a micro-gym. A million dollars isn't enough to retire on—not if you plan to live to 150. But what if I kept it alive, paid myself a salary of $100,000, and kept it forever? On the eleventh year, when I'd barely be fifty, I'd already have earned over a million dollars on the gym and done the same amount of work (none).

If this is a possibility, why would anyone sell their business at all?

But if you look for another example of the "cash flow asset" strategy applied to the service industry, you won't find one. No one else has successfully bridged this gap (in the fitness industry, at least.) And as I teach the strategy through our mentorship program, more and more gym owners reach the "retirement" point. And they're doing it far faster than I did. In some cases, they take less than three years from their opening date.

Three years from opening a business to wealth? That's incredible. That's like winning the lottery—except you control the odds and pick the numbers! It won't happen for most people that quickly, but it can happen. The reason it rarely happens is that most people aren't lucky enough to connect the two big ideas. I was in the right place at the right time and did.

My success created a platform of influence. But my authenticity (I shared every step, including the failures) created a platform of trust. And that's the platform on which Two-Brain Business became the largest mentoring agency in the fitness world.

At Two-Brain Business, we refer to the process of building this influence and trust the "Authority Ladder."

THE AUTHORITY LADDER

We coach thieves through the Authority Ladder to help them make a sustainable platform of wealth. It allows them to help more people and to help people more because they'll have more financial resources, more connections, and more knowledge to share. The steps to the Authority Ladder, in loose order, are:

- **Niche ID:** Create a clear definition of the person you wish to serve, to the exclusion of nonideal clients. Identify "seed" clients with the power to make decisions and purchases. Build a client list through email sign-ups, social media user harvesting, and landing pages.
- **Niche Survey:** Find which problems your seed clients

are trying to solve. Interview seed clients in person, testing different questions.

- **Top Challenge ID:** Using the lexicon of the seed clients, determine the best opportunities for your service to solve their problems. Measure affinity and pain ratio.
- **Power of 10 Marketing:** Create and publish content in various media (written, podcast, webinar, video, ebooks, etc.) to address the top challenges of the seed clients within the niche. Find the top ten problems and create ten pieces of content to answer each. Measure the response to each section of content (traffic, download frequency, website, and social media interaction, repetition, and questions at live events).
- **Book:** Produce and publish a book containing the best-received content from the Power of 10 Marketing exercise. For example, the top ten blog posts can form ten chapters in the book.
- **Webinar:** Audience discussion in a series of live webinars. Use the webinars to build an email list. Podcasts follow the same strategy (live audience engagement). Note which questions keep popping up and configure the content into click magnets.
- **Partnerships:** Move from incremental growth to geometric growth by sharing content and writing referral agreements with complementary partners. Broaden your platform by linking to theirs.
- **Courses:** Launch full courses on our hosted platform.

Build out an online "university" that answers user questions, teaches best practices, and solves problems in advance.

- **Mentorship:** Offer one-on-one access through monthly calls, group meetings, text, or email-based mentorship. Require an "incubator" period to ensure a common baseline, then an "accountability" period to work backward from specific goals.
- **Duplication:** Solve the "icon" problem by replacing yourself in the mentorship role with content. Train other mentors to assist.
- **Authority:** Continue to publish frequently, but broaden your content to widen the niche. What else can you offer the same audience? Consider that first.

Since many of these steps take years of persistent effort to fully develop, your focus will be on the rapid-growth opportunities that follow the initial steps. Some might overlap one another to generate cash flow as quickly as possible. And some steps might not be necessary (for example, writing and publishing a book). Reaching the "top" rung of the Authority Ladder isn't necessary for success in most cases. The ladder is more indicative of the order of business than the goal.

We work through the Authority Ladder in our mentoring program once the thief is ready to share what she's learned with her expanded audience. Many of our clients have published books, run seminars, or even built worldwide mentorship programs of their own. They're changing hundreds of lives and making hundreds of thousands—even millions—of dollars doing it. The best part: by following my path, they can do it so much faster than I ever did.

THE THIEF'S ROLES

In the Thief phase, the entrepreneur forms partnerships (horizontal connections) to bring his idea to new niches or forms mentorships (vertical connections) to help others within their niche. Or he might just sell the company and sit on the beach.

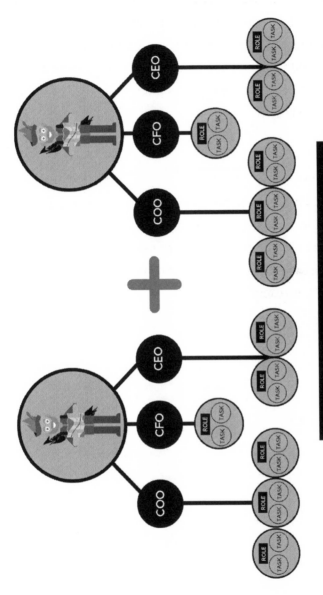

THIEF PHASE HIERARCHY

In the Thief phase, you might consider yourself chairman of the board, but you must limit your business interactions to those who sit at your table. You may find yourself tempted to respond to multiple tiers of staff requests, but do not give in. That separation is imperative to your transition to (and through) the Thief phase.

Most thieves limit their daily business conversation to five reports or fewer. This might mean a discussion with the CEO of one company or, if the thief still sits in the CEO chair, a conversation with the three meta roles (CFO, CSO, COO) of their primary business. Other reports might come from the thief's financial planner or a personal assistant or someone overseeing a specific project, but that's it.

This management layer will protect you from being drawn into daily operations or "fighting fires." It exists to be that buffer and to keep you focused on partnerships, investments, or new opportunities. If you're constantly drawn into the daily operation of your businesses, you will never fulfill your true role. "Retirement" means choosing where your attention goes, but it's not a one-time decision; it's a constant process.

As a thief, you'll always have to fight the temptation to meddle in your business instead of seeking new challenges. It's easier to question the team than to push yourself toward something new, easier to be a tyrant than to allow the team to make mistakes with your livelihood. But your attention should aim outward, not inward; up, not down.

THE THIEF'S SALES AND MARKETING PLAN

As a thief, you should no longer be involved in the business's sales and marketing. Those roles should exist as a division within the company (or group of companies) and fall under the purview of the CSO, held accountable to the revenue metrics mentioned in Part Three, "Tinker."

THE THIEF'S MENTOR

Accountability never ends. As a thief, you might not have a formal business mentor, but you'll still be accountable to someone—or maybe accountable to your deathbed. Use this guiding question: "When I'm on my deathbed, will I be able to list those I've served? Will I see the impact I've made? And what if I don't see that impact? Will I still be satisfied?"

A thief often keeps his own counsel. And that means learning to detach from praise or even thanks. It means self-satisfaction without acknowledgment. The final steps to self-actualization are always taken alone.

THE THIEF'S CHALLENGES

You may not be #grinding anymore. And you're probably more likely to live out your perfect day *every day* than to martyr yourself to your business. But the Thief stage will still carry its share of challenges.

WHO IS YOUR TRIBE?

"I'm so old, I don't even buy green bananas anymore," Wayne told me when we met. I laughed at the line. He was only seventy, and we exercised together for over a decade. He was one of my first informal mentors.

Wayne's a real entrepreneur. When McDonald's opened a location in communist Russia, Wayne was there. He owned a construction company and four McDonald's franchises. And every day, Wayne meets a group of other septuagenarians for lunch. All of them are business owners. And they often start new businesses. None of them needs the money, but they all need the stimulation. They build their new businesses as partners sometimes, but they always start with a succession plan because, well, none of them is buying green bananas anymore.

The stimulation keeps their minds sharp. It gives them a reason to get out of the house and think. Maybe they're gaining weight at their restaurant of choice, but Wayne works it off with me, and they often golf in the afternoons.

No one gives the others advice. They all give each other a hard time. They're all survivors. And while they watch their friends wither up and die, the members of Wayne's group are still sharp and physically fit. The group serves both as a stimulus and filter for its members.

Wayne understands that you are the average of your five closest relationships. Are those relationships pulling you toward greater wealth? Greater longevity? Are they challenging your mind, or are you merely putting in time?

The top challenge in the Thief phase is finding a pack of thieves to run with. A band of merry thieves is hard to find and must be cultivated for a long time, but it's important to surround yourself with people who pull you up and challenge you. Every fitness enthusiast knows the power of exercising in a pair or in a group. The greatest entrepreneur in the fitness space today is Greg Glassman, the founder of CrossFit, and he put it this way: "When I ride alone, my wheel is always in front." Riding with others who are faster will make you ride harder and go faster. The same happens in the gym, in business, and in life.

If you surround yourself with people who are more successful than you are, you will usually rise to their level. You will want to wear their clothes. You will want to match their donations. And you will adopt their habits and mindset.

For example, one of my favorite things about attending mastermind group meetings is that everyone in the room makes more money than I do. They wear nicer clothes, drive cool cars, and they think like millionaires because they are millionaires. When I'm in that group, I think like a millionaire too. I approach problems without my usual fear filters about money. I think on a grander scale. I dress better, feel better, and take comfort knowing others have faced the problems I do now.

When I'm with entrepreneurs who are still in the Farmer phase, though, I adopt their mindset. I worry about money and try to do all the tasks in my business myself. I chase every new opportunity without first asking, "Is this worth my time?"

Founders and farmers learn to cut low-value tasks from their day. Tinkers learn to cut low-value ideas. And thieves must learn to cut low-value interactions with people who hold them back, food that dulls their senses, and physical habits that blunt their lifespan. Surround yourself with other positive, healthy people, and you will solve many of the problems you'll encounter at the Thief phase.

PRIORITIZATION

With unlimited time (and boundless resources), it can

be hard for a thief to prioritize. Where will your service, knowledge, and funding make the most significant impact? Where will it have the most leverage?

Before you help your community, you must optimize your personal platform. Millions of dollars won't fix a struggling marriage, and many entrepreneurs' families show the wear of the years spent building the business. And since consistency, culture, and service are the pathway to joy, the entrepreneur must make sure he strengthens his family as much as his business:

- **Consistency:** Your family has to know you will be home at night and available to coach their soccer games.
- **Culture:** Your family must know, without a doubt, that you won't let work interfere with family time. That means stress, but it also means distraction.
- **Service:** Your family needs to know they come FIRST.

To help find the holes in your family base, I recommend the following exercises. Put yourself in a private place to do them. I've had many entrepreneurs break down on my shoulder while completing them.

The Twenty-Four-Hour Emergency

You've just discovered you have twenty-four hours to live.

You're dying of an incurable disease, but you can't tell anyone you have it because that's how it spreads.

First, whom would you want to see in the next twenty-four hours?

Second, what would you want to say to them?

Third, what would you want to share with the world?

Take time to answer the questions thoughtfully. Then return to complete the next section.

The Seven-Day Urgency

You've just discovered that you have seven days to live.

First, whom would you want to see in the next seven days?

Second, what would you want to say to them?

Third, what would you want to share with the world?

How are your answers different from the first time you did the exercise, with a twenty-four-hour window? Answer the questions. Then wait a day before returning to complete the next section.

Thirty-Day Importance

You've just discovered that you have thirty days to live.

Whom would you want to see in the next thirty days?

What would you want to say to them?

What would you want to share with the world?

Put It Together: Bubble Lists

When you're sorting your personal priorities, use a "bubble list" to help you decide where your attention belongs. This exercise works in emergency situations, but also on a day-to-day level to help you prioritize.

Begin with your thirty-day list. Read through all the items on your thirty-day list. If some are more urgent than others, put them at the top. Now, look at the first two items at the top of the list.

If you could only do ONE of those two things, which would it be? Put your choice at the top of the list. Now, look at the second and third items on the list. If you could only do ONE of the two, which would it be? Reorganize your list depending on the answer.

Next, look at the third and fourth items on your list, and then the fourth, fifth, and sixth, and so on. As you work through the list, your top priorities will "bubble up" to the top.

The best lists seem to contain only six to eight items. And few people work all the way through their lists each day or each month. But knowing which should take priority will help you focus your time, energy, and money.

BOREDOM

I started this section with this phrase: "You've made it. You can stop now." For many people, retirement means "finished." But not for entrepreneurs.

For entrepreneurs, retirement means, "This one is working! On to the next!" The greatest potential curse for an entrepreneur can also be a great gift. We'll never be done. We'll never retire. We'll never get bored.

Our parents retired to a couch or lounge chair. They let game show announcers ease them into their twilight years. The diseases of inactivity—diabetes, obesity, cognitive decline, osteoporosis—often shortened their lifespan. When their careers ended, they had nothing else to do. Their social lives, eating habits, and need to get up in the morning all disappeared.

Entrepreneurs who stay in the Founder phase—sometimes even in the Farmer phase—can fall into the same trap. They've bought themselves a job, and when they can sell that job to someone else, they don't have a career left.

But entrepreneurs who make it to the tinker and Thief phases have options. At forty-two, I'm "retired" from some of my companies, even though they continue to run profitably and pay me. It would be easy to fall into the same traps that sixty-five-year-olds do. Luckily, as an entrepreneur, I'm drawn to other projects. I've never watched less television in my life. I still get up at 4 a.m. to write.

Boredom is a killer. Entrepreneurs train their minds for decades to look for threats and respond. We exercise our amygdala until it's big and strong. Our bodies are on constant alert. When we take away those threats and challenges, our brains don't immediately reshape into retirement mode. They just look harder for serpents in the bushes.

We fight with our wives. We argue about politics. We get angry over baseball games. We backfill that brain space with stress and drama we've concocted because our brains abhor a vacuum. And since these things are mostly in our heads, our cognitive connections go down.

We become more stubborn and less intelligent. Without a real outlet for our stress, we internalize it. We eat our feelings. Our blood pressure goes up. We flood our cells with insulin until they become resistant. We get sick.

The path toward happiness and health is the path away from boredom. That means a lifelong dedication to entrepreneurship and service.

I ate lunch with a good friend and new retiree last week. She told me, "I'm so busy now I don't know how I ever fit my job into my schedule before!" She went on to tell me about the hobbies she's pursuing, the workouts she's doing, and what she's reading now. She also mentioned all the people she's meeting and how her social circle is expanding to replace the coworkers she no longer has. She's volunteering to help others. She's going to live a long time.

"Stay busy" is a platitude that almost every retiree hears. "Stay serving" might be the true path to a longer life.

FUNCTIONAL RETIREMENT

Age sixty-five: gold watch, couch, *The Price Is Right* on TV. Ahhhhh...

Not for the thief.

For the thief, retirement means cash flow without your presence. It means choice: Do I go into the office today, or not? Do I work from Florida or Nebraska? Do I need to be anywhere...or can I choose to write instead?

And that can happen at any age.

Kaleda Connell is twenty-nine and retired. Her story is on TwoBrain Radio here: https://twobrainbusiness.com/episode-141-founders-club/

Let me be clear here: Kaleda doesn't have to work anymore. Unless she wants to (she does).

Last summer, while sitting on a deck at a waterfront restaurant, I told my wife, "I think I'm going to retire in two more years."

She said, "Retire from what?"

She was referring to my lifestyle: I wake up when I want, write for a few hours, read books, ride my bike, and play with my kids. I coach their teams. I wear jeans and cargo shorts and t-shirts. I look like a retiree, except for the physical part. I look forty and feel thirty.

This is a dramatic change from me when I was actually thirty: I was burned out, broke, and exhausted. I had no clear path forward. I was aging fast: I looked thirty, acted forty, and felt like I was fifty. I found a mentor that I couldn't really afford. On my first visit, he asked me, "What scares you most right now?"

I said, "I'll never be able to retire."

He said, "You're not going to retire anyway. You LOVE to work. So stop worrying about it."

See, I knew "retirement" meant "enough money to stop worrying," but I thought it also meant old age and a pension of some kind. I didn't know that I could CONTROL money, build cash flow assets, and actually be the one to decide when to stop working.

A few years later, I listened to *Rich Dad, Poor Dad* on audiobook. I loved the idea of buying and holding. And it made me wonder, "Could this be done with a business? Could I really make my business something that pays me—even when I'm not there?"

The quest began. And I'm here to tell you: your business CAN. So can you.

This is functional retirement: the choice to work—or not—without sacrificing your income.

You can take "mini-retirements" of several months throughout your life, instead of just dropping off a cliff at the end.

You can make a near-passive income while you're young enough to travel.

You can coach your kids in the middle of the day without calling in a replacement or shipping your product late.

You can go watch the Tour de France while you're young enough to ride it. I'll probably go next year...but I don't have to decide right now, because I can just decide at the last minute.

I might decide to start another company instead (it's a bit of a habit). Or go somewhere else, or start writing another book. You can too, if you build your business to get you there.

Functional retirement doesn't mean living your best with the time you have left. It means creating a life that doesn't feel like work.

It's too late for me to be functionally retired at twenty-nine. Maybe it's too late for you to be functionally retired at forty-two. But is it too late for freedom at fifty? Maybe not.

THE THIEF'S CHECKLIST

There's no checklist in the Thief phase, but I want you to check IN with yourself regularly. Ask yourself:

- "Am I happy?" Don't settle for "happy enough."
- "Am I healthy?" Don't settle for "healthy enough."
- "Am I making a difference?" Don't settle for "making enough."

FINAL THOUGHTS

The path from founder to thief is the path to self-actualization. The founder builds a foundation of service, the farmer cultivates success, the tinker builds on her invention, and the thief spreads the wealth. Success isn't a guarantee in any phase, but mentorship can be a huge help, and that's why I've chosen to mentor other entrepreneurs.

Though I'd achieved the thief level with my first businesses, launching the Two-Brain Business mentorship program brought me right back down to the Founder phase again, but this time, I had the experience and wisdom to grow the business faster. I could leverage lessons learned while mopping the floor to negotiate deals worth millions of dollars.

When you open a business, your career changes to "entrepreneur," and you'll never go back to another job. Every business sows the seeds for the next. Even if this business goes bankrupt, you'll have the wisdom to run the next business better.

I was lucky. My early lack of knowledge wasn't fatal. But it was close. And the lessons I learned at the bottom are now my core value. To say it more plainly, the bulls**t I went through is now the fertilizer that makes my crops grow fast. The fast-growing crops allow me more time to tinker. And more tinker time means I can crack open more locks.

I am a thief because I started as a terrible founder.

I understand that service is part of the path to happiness because I was miserable.

I know that giving is the answer because I spent years scrambling to take enough.

I write every day. Sometimes it's hard; sometimes it pours out because I'm driven to share something important. My daily average hovers between 3,000 and 6,000 words. Stories are good for making points sticky; examples help to make the complex simpler to understand. But the important messages in business and leadership—and life—can always be distilled into a few words. Here's my best attempt to deliver the distillate:

- Ten words on mission: Missions survive when plans fail, and plans almost always fail. (That one's from my hero, Seth Godin. The rest are mine.)
- Nine words on values: Without your values, it's turtles all the way down.
- Eight words on gratitude: Find it. Feel it. Share it. Every day.
- Seven words on creativity: There's no such thing as writer's block.
- Six words on health: Most problems clear up by morning.
- Five words on motivation: Your time is running out.
- Four words on balance: This, too, shall pass.
- Three words on marketing: Come with me.
- Two words on leadership: Follow me.
- One word on life and business: Open.

ABOUT THE AUTHOR

CHRIS COOPER is the author of Two-Brain Business, *Two-Brain Business 2.0*, and *Help First*.

When his first business was nearly bankrupt in 2008, Chris sought a mentor and began chronicling his turn-around on a blog called DontBuyAds.com. After 400 blog posts, Cooper self-published his first book, *Two-Brain Business*, which has now sold more than 20,000 copies worldwide.

Now a mentor to hundreds of entrepreneurs, and a team of mentors spanning the globe, Cooper shares the tactics, habits, and strategies that work for entrepreneurs in each stage of ownership in *Founder | Farmer |Tinker | Thief.*

Made in the USA
Middletown, DE
06 June 2019